# Washed in the Hurricane

*poems for an
endangered paradise*

Stephen Wing

WASHED IN THE HURRICANE
*Poems for an Endangered Paradise*

Copyright © 2024 by Stephen Wing.
Book design by Stephen Wing.
All rights reserved.

*Contains no A.I. ingredients.*

ISBN-10: 0-9793907-3-7
ISBN-13: 978-0-9793907-3-9

Wind Eagle Press
P.O. Box 5379, Atlanta GA 31107

PHOTO CREDITS

*front cover, top:* Hurricane Jeanne, 2004
*middle:* Brooklynn Long, age 5 – Andrea Zoppo
(Note: Brooklynn is now ten and already
an award-winning poet at her school.)

*back cover, background* – Kathryn Schambach
*author headshot* – Luz Wright

*for my mother*

Carol Ann Wise Wingeier

*who took me camping
when I was too young
to say no*

## Acknowledgements

With gratitude to:

*Cobalt Review* for publishing "View from a Mountain Ridge" and "Firmly Planted"

*EcoTheo Review* for publishing "Call to Worship"

*The Lake Claire Clarion* for publishing "Praising the Rain" and "Farewell, Blackbird Hotel," and for reprinting "View from a Mountain Ridge"

*Communities Magazine* for publishing "Lightning's Compass" "Grasshopper Man, Driving Through," and "The Writer on His Bicycle," and for reprinting "Praising the Rain"

Georgia Poetry in the Parks for publishing "Underfoot"

*Blue Milk* for publishing "Hurtling Through Darkness"

## Also by Stephen Wing

*Four-Wheeler & Two-Legged: Poems*
(Southeastern Front, 1992)

*Crossing the Expressway: Poems from the Open Road*
(Dolphins & Orchids, 2001)

*Proof of the Miraculous:*
*Campfire Poetry from the Rainbow Gatherings*
(Wind Eagle Press, 2018; out of print)

*Wild Atlanta: Greenspaces &*
*Nature Preserves of 'The City in the Forest'*
with photographs by Luz Wright
(Wind Eagle Press, 2023)

The Earth Poetry chapbook series:
*A Country Beyond All Borders: Poems for the Trees*
*As Above, So Below: Poems for the Water*
*To the Animal Tribes: Poems for the Animals*
*Under the Pavement: Poems for the Land*
*House of the Sky: Poems for a Living Planet*
(Wind Eagle Press)

*Honk If You're Awake! Poems for a Republic in Peril*
(Wind Eagle Press, 2026)

## Advance Reader Comments

"Stephen Wing's 'Earth Poetry' links careful observations of nature with a sense of the sacred through an appreciation of the way 'spirit and matter mingle and interplay' . . . The manifesto that concludes the book offers insights into our damaged and dangerous relationship to the natural world. . . . Wing provides dozens of powerful examples of what environmentally aware, environmentalist poetry might be, and might accomplish."

*Joel J. Brattin, professor of English, Worcester Polytechnic Institute*

"In Stephen Wing's poems, you will find soft-spoken conversations with the natural world, threads of ancient mystery, yearning for what's lost and hope for what remains. . . . His is a vital perspective, and one we can all share— without going to the wilderness or crossing the sea or orbiting the planet— just by paying attention to the nature that lingers all around us. It is telling us something."

*Wade Harrison, forester, writer, land conservation professional*

"Wing's poetry vividly reminds us not only that nature is beautiful— and some of the choices we humans have made much less so— but also that the lines we create to separate nature from technology, or humanity from the animals, or civilization from wilderness, really exist only in our dualistic minds. To top it off, the book ends with Wing's 'Earth Poetry' manifesto, a beautiful and brilliant statement about just why poetry like this is so vital and necessary for our time."

*Carl McColman, author of* Eternal Heart *and* Unteachable Lessons

"Wing lists Robinson Jeffers, Theodore Roethke, Kenneth Rexroth, Denise Levertov, Galway Kinnell, James Wright, W.S. Merwin, Gary Snyder, Wendell Berry, and Mary Oliver as the 'tribal elders' from whom he learned his craft. My judgment is that with this collection, Wing earns for himself a place in any such list of importantly earth-wise American poets."

*Jim Allen, former English professor and published poet*

"The crisis of our time is that we're on-deck in these last moments when something, anything, can perhaps be done to slow the demise of our planet . . . Stephen Wing, as a responsible poet, lays out the ways we can re-calibrate our relationship to this world while continuing to honor its nurturing soul. . . . As Wing correctly notes, 'Everything you do . . . touches the wild world.' We can only hope our touch is as loving as these poems."

*Rupert Fike, author of* Lotus Buffet *and* Hello the House

# Table of Contents

*Introduction* — 9

### 1. Where the River Lives — 11

Edge of the Silence — 12
A Country Beyond All Borders — 14
Ducking Under Rainbows — 15
Treehugged — 16
Trees Are My Eldest Relatives — 17
Hunter-Gatherer — 20
The Heartwood of This Life — 21
Twilight in the Meadow — 22
Moonwalk — 24
Lightning's Compass — 24
Rhododendron Palace — 25
Where the River Lives — 26
Waking Up Outside — 27
The Babble of the Oracle — 28
Homeward — 29
Twig — 29
Paddlestroke — 30
Wingbeat — 31
Sleeplessly — 31
Whitewater Falls — 32
Wind in the Pines — 33
A Mouthful of Words — 33
Call to Worship — 34
Shadows on the Tent — 35
Cicadas — 36
The Art of Hiking — 36
View from a Mountain Ridge — 37
Postcard from the Wilderness — 38
Riverbank Meditation — 39
If This Page Were a Window — 40

| | |
|---|---|
| Unsurprised by Rain | 42 |
| Dusk | 43 |
| Wild Ocean | 44 |
| Underfoot | 44 |
| The Writer on Foot | 45 |

## 2. This Side of the Glass — 47

| | |
|---|---|
| Into the Immensity | 48 |
| All the Way Up | 49 |
| Ever Since Evolution | 50 |
| This Side of the Glass | 51 |
| Farewell, Blackbird Hotel | 52 |
| For Lack of Evidence | 54 |
| The Naked Scientist | 55 |
| Grandmother's Seeds | 56 |
| Lost Leaf | 57 |
| Native Blood | 58 |
| Asphalt Nights | 59 |
| The Country I Love Has No Flag (Only Blossoms) | 60 |
| Ten Years Eaten by the World | 62 |
| A Glance Before Drinking | 63 |
| River Blues | 64 |
| Man Breathing Life into Metal | 65 |
| Moth | 66 |
| Microtrash | 67 |
| Lord of the Intersection | 68 |
| Where You Fell | 69 |
| Hawk in the Warehouse | 70 |
| Praising the Rain | 72 |
| Visitors from the Sky | 73 |
| The Earth Forgives Everyone in the End | 76 |
| Marginalia | 77 |

| | |
|---|---|
| Daylight Calling | 78 |
| The Stones Cry Out | 79 |
| Grasshopper Man, Driving Through | 80 |
| The Writer on His Bicycle | 81 |

## 3. Hurtling Through Darkness — 83

| | |
|---|---|
| House of the Sky | 84 |
| The Deer That Flew | 86 |
| Dry Season | 87 |
| Bundle of Bones | 88 |
| Effortlessly Uphill | 89 |
| Distant Singing | 91 |
| The Graveyard of Empires | 92 |
| Inscription Found Among the Ruins | 94 |
| Washed in the Hurricane | 95 |
| The Enemy Logo | 101 |
| The Dividends of Sin | 102 |
| Understood | 104 |
| Hurtling Through Darkness | 106 |
| Carcasses Rusting in a Field | 107 |
| Spirals of Fire | 108 |
| Because We Believe | 110 |
| Pushing the Peace Bus | 112 |
| Daybreak at Eleven | 113 |
| Wildlife Opening | 114 |
| Firmly Planted | 115 |
| To Be Human | 116 |
| The Writer on the Freeway | 117 |

## 4. Earth Poetry: A Manifesto — 119

About the Author — 141

# INTRODUCTION

Allow me to introduce myself. I am a poet by vocation, 67 years old, born and raised right here on Planet Earth. "Stephen Wing" is my pen name, and something more. My father's name is *Wingeier*, from the Schweizer-Deutsch language of Switzerland. In English it means "eagle" or "vulture," depending on which Swiss person you ask. Legally that is my name too, but many years ago my father graciously gave me his consent to change the name I go by in the world. So *Wing* is the name I have chosen not just for writing, but for living.

Though at the time I only vaguely grasped why, I chose a name that originated not in the human realm but in the world of nature. Like every poet I write poems of many kinds, on many subjects, but one particular sub-genre has gradually taken on form and substance beneath my feet to become a spiritual path of sorts: poetry that links the human and natural worlds, reminding me that they are not two worlds after all, but one.

If it seems like a stretch to liken the writing of poems to a religious or personal discipline such as yoga, meditation, or devotion to a guru, look around. How did we reach a point in human evolution where our ways of life and livelihood now threaten irreversible damage to the biosphere we depend on to survive?

We got here by forgetting what our indigenous forebears understood: *life on Earth is itself a spiritual path*. Our everyday choices as individuals are moral choices, forks in that path; the same is true for our choices as a society. Every person's life and vocation is a spiritual path, whether we are aware of it or not.

Long ago certain ancestors of ours innocently chose a promising fork in the path called "civilization." That path gradually left behind traditional indigenous religion, with its sense of a moral responsibility to the rest of Creation. Eventually it left religion behind completely, and then morality itself, to became a purely secular path. We have now reached the inevitable endpoint of that trajectory, where under a secular doctrine called "economics," amoral and even immoral choices win the highest honors and rewards among both individuals and societies.

Poets are supposed to be observers, not commentators; witnesses, not advocates; aesthetes, not activists. Taking sides is against the rules of academic detachment. But we live in a desperate time, when the future of human civilization depends on each and every human finding a way to help change its course. Even the poets. Or, perhaps, *especially* the poets.

*Stephen Wing*

Said the river: I am part of holiness.
And I too, said the stone. And I too, whispered
the moss beneath the water.

Mary Oliver, "The River Clarion"

# (1)
# Where the River Lives

## Edge of the Silence

Climbing the mountain
into the fog
long after midnight,
I wind up slowing down
almost to zero,
straddling the double yellow
center line
between my headlights
just to see the road...

Then I cross
the Gilmer County line
at the top of the ridge
— every scrap of fog suddenly
gone!

*This road winds up
into the time before anyone had bothered
to invent a wheel,
let alone contrive
a set of notched and interlocking wheels
into a clock*

Accelerate through the curves,
coast the downgrades,
tires slipping side to side
in slick mud, clinging to the gravel...

Curling up
across the folded-down seats
under the eaves of the forest
and the spiraling stars,
I finally reach the edge
of the silence

The crickets have
waited up for me

*In all the pre-Columbian Americas,*
*not one wheeled artifact*
*ever found*
*except for children's toys*

The last half-hour of the journey
I go on foot,
    up a trail of sorts
through open woods and morning
        sunlight
toward the crest of the ridge,
looking for a clear view
    and the right pair of trees
to hang my hammock,
        circling
with a hawk
    on a mountain thermal
right on up
        into the sky—

*Into the time before anyone*
*ever looked down from a mountain*
*and imagined lines*
*across a map*

## A Country Beyond All Borders

Balancing on a footbridge of lashed poles,
hanging on to a handrail of rope,
I am crossing more than just a creek
and the miniature gorge it has dug
through the slow-trickling centuries.

I am stepping over the frontier
of light and shadow, crossing
an ancient threshold in my brain,
entering the sovereign territory of the trees.

Behind me in the sunny meadow,
artifacts of my own time lie scattered
in the weeds, rusting metal and fading ink,
relics of restless imagination
and intricate engineering
left where their usefulness ended.

On this side the treetrunks stand
in mysteriously random order,
their branches above me like rippling flags
of foliage, part earth, part wind,
their leaves underfoot like a carpet of memories.

I have left behind a familiar country
of geometric blacktop
to follow the crooked logic of water
cutting through yellow clay
as we meander together downstream.

Even the sky that gazes down between the leaves
contemplates me with a wild
furtive intelligence, nothing like
the imperial burst of daylight back there
in the civilized open.

The trees are small, barely older
than the next generation of loggers,
still colonized by plastic ribbons
and blazed with blue paint:
but in one long, slow breath I fill myself
with a half-remembered quiet, and feel them
open their lofty limbs
to take me in.

Here and there, like bright scars
among the patches of moss
and fallen branches, lonesome bits of trash
beg to be gathered up and carried home.

### Ducking Under Rainbows

Young trees
arching over the trail
mark the spectrum
of a quieter, humbler rainbow,
closer to the ground,
one shade of green
giving way to the next
as I pass under
heading for my tent

Then a low branch I hadn't noticed
taps on my hatbrim,
knocks my cap onto the path
behind me, calling me home
to this moment I'm
striding through
just when my thoughts
begin to wander off

# Treehugged

The last time I hugged a tree,
it was an accident.
I was reaching around its rough bark
with my rope,
bent on stretching and securing
my tarp before dark,
while my other hand crept
the other way,
groping for the dangling end
like a tailor
measuring a wooden mannequin,
when I caught a sudden
scent: sharp, damp,
unmistakably the smell
of living flesh
half an inch from my nose.
My fingers met,
I grasped the rope, but held on
for a moment
to her matronly waist,
enjoying
her gracious embarrassment,
my own shy
boldness,
the life that flows
in my veins and hers.
No, I take it back—
the last time
I hugged a tree
it was
a surprise,
but no accident.

## Trees Are My Eldest Relatives

### 1.

Trees frame a different picture of the world
than a window

Their limbs reach up and out like a hundred
crooked paths into the sky

Their roots reach into dark places I never knew
belonged to me

Their budding breaks the silence of winter
with innocent music

Their leaves drop to cover the ground with summer's
empty skin

Their bark hides a network of vessels and nerves
and deep, slow thoughts

Their swaying draws an everchanging map
of the wind's migrations

Their rotting fallen trunks feed the offspring
of all species equally

2.

Humans climb trees to commune
with our higher selves
among the galaxies of leaves

Humans amputate branches
to clear an unswerving path
for powerlines and pulses of data

Humans hang sheetrock over studs
to cover a deep-rooted yearning
for our original forest home

Humans grind whole forests into pulp
for a one-day supply
of toilet paper and newsprint

Humans harvest the nuts and fruits of trees
to plant the seeds of photosynthesis
in our dark bellies

Humans hug trees to hold on to something
that hasn't yet blown away
in the desert sandstorm of civilization

Humans plant trees to disguise
our naked loneliness and grief
on a planet of clearcuts and pavement

Humans breathe in the exhalations of trees
day and night just to stay alive,
and rarely look up to say thanks

3.

The trees are my eldest relatives,
towering above the sidewalk like grownups
at the playground, silent amid the chatter
and bickering of humankind

Old-growth climax forests
manufacture topsoil and generate rain,
shelter the delicate web of root-hairs and mycelia
that weave the living world

Cruel empires have fallen one by one
when they cut down the last of their woodlands
to build fleets of battleships
and feed the smelters for weaponry

Trees talk to me in a syntax of scented breezes
which my lungs comprehend as oxygen
and my eyes translate into wild
branching beauty

Their quiet contemplation of sunlight and rain,
birth, illness, old age and death
tells me all I need to know to outlive
the daily presentiment of dying

## Hunter-Gatherer

All I'm hunting
is firewood,
but suddenly I catch a whiff
of the prehistoric thrill
of closing in on my prey—
a long straight piece of hardwood
slanting up across my path
where two standing trunks caught it
waist-high off the ground,
way too long to carry
till I balance it over a downed log
and bare the teeth
of my sawblade— triumphantly
bearing the cut lengths home
across my shoulder
for my clan and tradition,
for my Paleolithic
ancestors, for the family
fire...

      *Gazing*
*into the age-old oracle of the flames*
*hours later*
*I can almost read the heat*
*rising off the coals,*
                *matter*
*flickering into energy,*
*sequestered carbon*
*on the sacrificial pyre,*
*devouring oxygen, gushing smoke,*
*rekindling sunlight*
*through the winter night*

## The Heartwood of This Life

Gazing down through the woods at sunset
into that green
infinity of trees between trees between trees,
I catch just a glimpse
of a distant horizon somewhere
inside

like that black gap
between the farthest, faintest specks of stars
which you know must be
exploding with light
if your earthbound eyes could only see that
far—

There
through the webwork of twigs and branches
in the waning light,
amid the green and yellow mosaic of leaves, I see
deepest:

Every breath I take
and return
exchanges something vital with the forest,
every beat of my pulse
springs from the same heart
that spins this pinwheel
galaxy

as I stand here gawking, motionless, lost
in the rising twilight,
the greyblue boundary of afternoon and evening,
the bright split heartwood of this
life

## Twilight in the Meadow

Back in my old
tent spot, a quarter-turn of the year
past the blaze of summer,
and I've got my camp set up
just in time for the show: twilight
drifting in
among the autumn trees.

Spreading my blanket
in the dry leaves
to make a passable front porch,
I settle down crosslegged and look out
across the overgrown meadow
in the waning light.

Insects and frogs begin to sing
as the day slowly
seeps away, and I join in.
Not that I can chirp, chitter or peep:
my part in the choral arrangement
is to listen
and take notes.

Above the dark ridge, the sky
still holds its light—
distant glitter of stars, hint
of imminent moon, disembodied glow
of another world somewhere
beyond the treeline—
as if that enormous mass of air
were solid light, the mountain
a yawning vacuum...

It takes a certain effort
to remain still,
at least as motionless as the world
breathing around me.

But by carefully not paying attention,
I can let myself float along
through this endless
abiding moment when the day steps
imperceptibly
into the world between.

And suddenly a flock of words
is fluttering around me,
singing their crude but earnest imitations
of the wild song of the woods,
and I'm hungrily snatching them
out of the air,
scribbling them down
on my dim, vanishing notepad:

*nightfall ... moonrise ...*
*no such thing as solitude*
*in this buzzing, swaying, rustling crowd*

The daylight disappears so gradually
into darkness
that it's impossible to remember
that light and dark are two
different things
as we've all been taught, let alone
opposites ...

Reading in the woods by flashlight
deep into the night
is like traveling on a bus
through a nocturnal forest
that teems with life, gazing the whole time
into dark glass at a brightly lit
mirror of the human world.
I snap off the light
and look up: the meadow
sketched in charcoal,
awash in moon.

## Moonwalk

I came to a place
where the moonlight lay sprawled
across the path.
The path was only an old gravel road
interrupted every so often
by miniature lakes
filled with muddy water,
but under the moon
and the branches of shadow
it shimmered
with a quiet beckoning,
a silvery whisper,
a doorway into stillness where I paused
a moment and
stepped
into a cold pool of light.


## Lightning's Compass

With every flash and flicker of the sky,
I glimpse another few steps
of the trail back to my tent,
this slow pilgrimage between the trees
without a flashlight—
fork to the left, jog to the right,
slippery downgrade, low-hanging branch—
like my life sometimes,
the chain of epiphanies lighting up my path
and the pitch-dark
between

## Rhododendron Palace

Even the sunlight is green down here
between the green walls
of this rhododendron palace
with its green-tinted water
and a tinge of green on all the rocks,
its crowd of tangled limbs
reaching out with waxy green fingers—
down here
                  where the trail
crosses the river and the river winds out
toward the windy lake
while our boat sits rocking
on the mutual reflection
of water and light.
                        Only later
in the spring, when this entire cove bursts
into flaring pink flowers
will it become blindingly apparent
what all those green limbs and fingers
were reaching out for . . .
                            And if,
for some unforeseeable reason
we should happen to come back
to witness it, would it
occur to us to wonder
what our own awkward
fumbling fingers are reaching for
when we stretch
toward the intangibles that wait,
hidden somewhere inside us,
to blaze up
                into blossom?

## Where the River Lives

The cicadas singing out there
in the dark
don't have to compete with the rumble and honk
of the highway across the river.
They sing only for each other.
It's up to me which station I tune in as I lie here
in my tent
not yet ready to sleep.

Next morning, following a dry gully
down the rounded flank
of the hill behind my campsite, I make my pilgrimage
to the river.

The terrain slopes gently, gradually steeper, finally
almost vertical.
Inching across a tangle of fallen logs,
I drop at last to a floodplain of tall grass and a beach
of unpolished pebbles: the wild,
elusive place
where the river lives.

Through a gap in the trees upstream I see flashes
of that other constant flow
that kept me awake last night, my old friend
Interstate 85, hurrying diligently,
feverishly by.

I stand at the river's edge
where the lacy fringe of current slips
between the pebbles
under my shoes.
Dip both hands into its warm, swift, shallow flow
to bathe my face.
Sit down on a log temporarily stranded here
by the last flood. Open my book.
Sit here drinking in
the river's own opinionated
version of the story.

## Waking Up Outside

Sunrise in the mountains
always begins somewhere
on the other side
                of the mountain
whose shadow you slept in

*Everything is uphill from a river, even
back home in the city
though I never noticed
where the sloping streets were gently
leading me*
                until I awoke
on this wild riverbank

Waking up outside always
changes you
                inside
the way all the colors change
when the sun comes out,
even down here under the trees

*This is a vision I had
one morning
and walked around in for a while
before I noticed it wasn't
going away*
                Clouds
mirror the mountain skyline

## The Babble of the Oracle

At the exact instant I lost track,
the chatter in my head
merged with the rippling quiet of the stream
making its way down the mountain,
keeping everything along its path
alive— moss, ferns, crawdads,
rhododendron and dogwood and pine—
while simultaneously
sculpting the rocks, supervising
the redistribution of sediment,
conjoining with runoff
from other watersheds downstream
to eventually converge
in a massive, majestic, twisting and gliding
serpent of riverwater,
flowing finally into the vast global
conglomerate of waters—
a sparkling bridge
from the mountain to the sea,
doing its part in the conspiracy of elements
to maintain the balance
of living chemistries
while incidentally keeping me too
hydrated and alive, its single
wordless answer
to every possible question
returning me now by slowly retreating
degrees of wonder to this damp seat
on a fallen log
spanning the babble of the oracle
in this exact
endlessly flowing
instant

## Homeward

I travel the creekbed
doing my best
to keep up with the stream,
stepping from moss to rock to moss
down a staircase of tumbled boulders,
clambering over logs whose bark
has rotted away in the mist,
doubling over on all fours
through the thickets of rhododendron,
vaulting little pools and waterfalls
chasing nothing but *downstream,
downstream—*
                            Then I reach
the road, and remember I was lost.
Ninety degrees: left or right? I choose
uphill.
              The water goes
singing on homeward without me.


## Twig

Lugging
a five-gallon jug of water
along the path beside the stream,
I notice a twig
riding the glassy ripple of current
beside me, keeping pace
without effort, and suddenly
it's the water that carries me

## Paddlestroke

It's easy: just
reach ahead
and pull the paddleblade back
through the resistance
and the give
of the water beside you.
Pull with everything you've got,
every muscle
in your entire body, every ounce
of willpower you own.
Then lift, rest
a fraction of a second,
and do exactly the opposite
on your other side.  Then repeat
and repeat again,
striving self-consciously for rhythm
till it becomes as constant
and irresistible as breathing.
Don't stop.
Don't look ahead
at the blue distance between the islands
or glance left or right
at the shoreline
expecting to see progress.
Watch the water gliding past
with every paddlestroke
as the bow of the kayak surges ahead.
Watch the light
whirling in the eddies
as the paddleblade enters
and slips through.
Keep going.
Don't stop.

## Wingbeat

I woke
to see the muscle in a loon's wing
as it rose and flexed in front of my canoe:
no creature of mere feather,
black and grey-striped ghost
afloat in its reflection, suddenly
it stood up on the water,
spread its wet white underfeathers to the sun,
took three steps back, and I could see
the solid brawn beneath
each wingbeat.

I broke my stride in mid-stroke
and sat still, breathless
as the floating loon before me
while my heart still swam a beat behind
in its slow-settling
reflection.

## Sleeplessly

Listening
to the lake
out there in the dark,
cold black depths shifting
sleeplessly
under the moon,
I lie awake in my tent
riding the dark toss and turn
of the waves.

## Whitewater Falls

This is where ancient people
came to worship:
I can see it in the eyes
of the people I pass on the asphalt path
heading back to their cars
as the roaring through the trees
rises steadily to a crescendo
and it comes suddenly
into view—
              This is what
ancient people came here to worship,
I can see: not the water itself,
or the constant thunder
of its falling, not even the unseen
power that makes it fall—
that god nowadays
known as "gravity"— but the nameless deity
that lives in human awe,
the wonder that each of us unknowingly
carries inside until we round
a bend in the path and see
through a gap in the foliage
who that booming voice
belongs to—
              But this, I can see,
is why ancient people came
to worship here: this ceaseless flow
out of the looming escarpment
of the Blue Ridge, crashing down
from its towering cliff
into the depths it has hollowed
out of solid granite
over millennia, an irrefutable truth
utterly independent of me
and my kind, world without end,
amen.

## Wind in the Pines

The wind roars in the pines
The pines rock
              in the wind

I snap off the brittle grey-bleached
branches of fallen pines
to coax the heavy slabs of split oak
into flame
              A storm of sparks
swarms up on the wind
like fledgling stars eagerly
leaving the nest

I unzip the front door
of my tent, then the back door
and let the wind
              roar through


## A Mouthful of Words

Like a mouthful of words
leaking out
into the world,
the wind plays its flute
of needles and leaves,
the stream plays its
rocky violin,
the blackbirds line up
on the powerlines
and pass along the latest
gossip
and the oldest of philosophies.

## Call to Worship

Whenever I'm ready to grieve
or slow to marvel
I remember this land as I've
never seen it,
the way it must have looked
a thousand years before I opened
my astonished infant's eyes—

*The rising chorus of ridges,*
*treeline after treeline, climbing*
*to the misty edge of Creation.*
*The waterfall tumbling back down*
*in a clear cold rush.*

Before the invention of wilderness
or the need for churches,
when every bush blazed in the sunrise,
in the time before time that inspired
the myth of heaven—

*Nothing but forest and sky,*
*wet leaves dripping after a rain.*
*Nectar of unforbidden fruit.*
*Stained glass at sunset*
*without a window.*

Before the need for gardens
or the invention of fences,
before one piece of the Garden
was fenced off
and deeded over to "Eden"—

*Rivers winding*
*through the shady nave of the trees.*
*Cathedral columns of light.*
*A host of insects chanting endless*
*praise.*

Before anyone needed a pulpit higher
than the lowliest toadstool,
when every weed was medicine
and all medicines were sacred gifts
of the soil—

Whispering ghosts of people
and the other
animals who lived here then
grieve with me as I gaze around
at what the world has become . . .

Then I meet an infant,
who teaches me
with wide-open eyes
how to marvel again
at the quiet sanctuaries of green
that persist
between all these
roads and wires and signs.


## Shadows on the Tent

An inchworm on a blade of grass,
the blade bending, the worm
arched and reaching
from its bent tip,
searching air and sunlight
for something beyond its knowing,
pure faith in the world
underfoot—

## Cicadas

What a racket the cicadas make
calling back and forth
across the darkness between them!
What can it mean?
Because I've learned that nothing
in this world lacks meaning,
except sometimes
the utterances of human lips
and vocal cords, and even then
only when they call into
this darkness that divides them
instead of across.


## The Art of Hiking

Who would walk all the way
down through the woods
to the bank of this
quiet little stream
and leave this empty can?

*The Tao that can be named*
*is not the Tao*

*The sign of great art*
*is to appear effortless*

*The purpose of cleaning*
*is to erase all evidence*

*The whole point of hiking*
*to the heart of any wilderness,*
*no matter how small,*
*is to leave no sign*

## View from a Mountain Ridge

"Mom," I ask on the way to the car,
"Do you remember hiking with me
on the Appalachian Trail?"
Single file, step by step along the ridgeline
of Blood Mountain, three days
to walk ten miles, Mom leading the way
with a hiking stick in each hand, one long
leisurely conversation, long overdue—
the trail winding between prehistoric
outcrops of granite, climbing and descending
through a luminous wilderness,
wild forest falling away on either side
on steep leaf-shadowed slopes
in green-tinted sunlight—
cooking breakfast and dinner in doll-size
aluminum pans over her tiny propane stove,
camping one night in a shelter
of rough-hewn stone and weathered beams,
the next in her cramped pup tent
in a dry wash below the trail
among rocks and roots and fallen leaves,
the most level place we could find—
That was seven years ago,
when Mom was seventynine,
and everything's changed now, except
once again I match my steps to hers
as we cross the parking lot
hand in hand, headed for the car
to visit Dad in the hospital after his bypass,
and she looks at me in one of her
flashes of lucidity, without blinking,
as if through a momentary gap
in drifting early morning mist,
without even a heartbeat's
hesitation, her voice clear and firm, declaring,
"The highlight of my life!"

## Postcard from the Wilderness

You know you've really
seen the wilderness
when it wakes up something wild
inside you,
something shy and fearless
that gazes out from a thorny lair
behind your eyes
at the headlights and billboards
of your journey home—

*because everything you do*
*whether choice or habit*
*touches the wild world,*
*sends ripples dancing across*
*the glassy light of the lake*

You'll know you have finally
discovered the wilderness
when you bring it home with you
and it builds a nest
in the highest branches of your
imagination,
inhabiting your silences,
your hungers, your wanderings
and homecomings,
your focused attention and
spontaneous laughter—

*because nothing we do*
*escapes the world of consequence,*
*chemicals leach from plastic*
*and the osprey's egg*
*cracks open too soon*

You'll get back
to the woods someday,
it doesn't matter when, you know it
deep in every muscle and bone,
doesn't matter at all
when the wilderness
hibernates all winter inside you,
breathing its hot musk
deeper than blood-vessels,
bone-marrow,
deeper than dreaming—

*because any time you close your eyes
the mountains loom above that
icy lake, the osprey circles overhead
and you're still there, wild
and alive*

## Riverbank Meditation

My attention floats
like the plastic bottle caught
in the crotch of a tree
that has toppled into the current,
still hanging on to the bank,
rippling the fast brown
smooth-sliding surface of the river
while a black bird croaks
its obsessive caw and
a human somewhere close by
compulsively
shoots off firecrackers
or bullets

## If This Page Were a Window

*"Everything that lives is holy,"*
wrote William Blake
in one of his gloomy
fits of rapture, gazing out
through a grimy window
across the brick and coal-smoke
of a muddy London street
into Paradise—

So why on Earth
would the deer
or the blacksnake
or the snowy owl even notice
the wild beauty
unscrolling endlessly around them
when they themselves
are each simply
one of its perfect, autonomous
moving parts?

*"But now ask the beasts
And they shall teach you,
And the fowls of the air,
And they shall teach you,"*
wrote the unknown scribe
of the Book of Job.
*"Or speak to the Earth,
and it shall teach you . . ."*

So why on Earth
wouldn't all those millions
of reverent readers
of that Holy Book
stop right there,
lift their eyes from the page
and glance out through
the nearest pane of window-glass
where every stray weed
and random pigeon out there
pecking at the dirt
only wait to be asked?

*"Try telling yourself*
*you are not accountable*
*to the life of your tribe*
*the breath of your planet,"*
wrote Adrienne Rich,
remembering a glance
more transparent than glass
she once exchanged
with the world, miles
from the nearest window—

So why do we forget to ask
the one place known
among the multitude of galaxies
to hoot and buzz and howl
and whistle with life
what life is for,
and why it has chosen us
to share in this
incomparable gift, and how
we might accomplish
that holy task?

## Unsurprised by Rain

It's Solstice everywhere,
north and south of the Equator
all the way to the Poles,
but here in the meadow
the grey light of the shortest day
is waning
as the grey shadow
of the rain
begins to lift

*No wonder they thought*
*of a Goddess*
*as they walked among the constellations*
*of glittering droplets*
*beading the wet branches*

The trees here
dress in a patchwork of greys
and greens,
wearing their lichen spots
and fringes of moss, evergreen
thick among the hardwood,
soft bark
damp and fertile
as the earth itself

*No wonder they conceived a God*
*watching the stars turn,*
*calculating the exact*
*degree of the Solstice, the moment*
*of Equinox*

Looking around at the trees
on the rising slopes
in the dusk, I feel
like a very small child gazing up
at the looming mountain
of Mama, incapable
of imagining
she could ever go
away

*My first duty is*
*to the Creation, to give back*
*what I have taken*
*and a little bit more, to repay*
*the sacrifices my ancestors made,*
*striving with head and heart*
*to hand something worthwhile on*
*to all these little ones*


## Dusk

Dusk.
I turn my back to the fire,
walk to the edge
of the meadow,
stand there among the trees
at the edge of the forest,
gazing in.
This is where the world
began
and here it begins
again.

## Wild Ocean

Wild ocean
like the sheen on the
> shoulder of a crow
> dipping and
>> gliding with the gulls—

not a shell left unbroken on the whole beach

## Underfoot

Every time I walk down
into the hollow
through the winter woods
or up the mountain again,
I stop right here.
Standing on the packed earth
of an old logging road
where the creek slips quietly
through its rusty culvert
underfoot,
I'm not so much listening as feeling
a kind of tickling caress
through the soles of my shoes
and I recognize
a crossing of paths, a choice,
a way back
if I could only turn
and follow.

## The Writer on Foot

If you want to know where
the muscles for walking are,
just do a little too
much of it

Stepping out
across the surface of the Earth,
you enter deeply, instantly
into full immersion
in the ocean of elements,
into unconditional air,
the cool caress of the grass
between your toes, crisp
fallen leaves crackling underfoot,
even the bare dirt
quivering, alive
beneath your living touch...

Thank you, Mother, for the blessing
of this holy sprinkle
of rain, this frog
serenade, the naked young moon
slipping shyly
between the clouds—

As the crickets' soft autumn hum
is to us,
so are we to the trees

as are they

to the rocks and the hills.

*Gary Snyder, "Little Songs for Gaia"*

# (2)
## This Side of the Glass

## Into the Immensity

When you grow weary at last
of changing channels,
just turn off the world and step
outside.

      But beware:
to step through that door is to risk
an encounter with the looming
immensity
we have built our little lives on.

A mountain river racing along
below the highway,
wave upon wave
of mountain ridges fading into mist
and distance—
The unfathomable ocean
or prairie horizon
swallowing the sun—

The immensity above us
with its vertigo of endless
emptiness,
its halo of stars, daylight as wide
as the wind—
The immensity below with its dark
casket of gravity,
the solid mystery of bedrock,
a molten heart
throbbing deep in the ground—

The turning planet itself,
swarming
with inarticulate life,
the vast humming intelligence
that sustains it all—
The majestic indifference
that was here
before we came and spins on
after we're gone—

And most of all,
whatever you do, don't
gaze too long
into the cavernous
immensity
that sleeps and sometimes
dreams
inside you.

## All the Way Up

Fall oaks towering
over church spires
and powerlines

Lone hawk circling
above the skyline

Pale winter sky soaring
higher yet

My wild gaze reaches
all the way up
and gathers it all in

## Ever Since Evolution
### for Dawn Aura

Of all that's ever
begun with an orgasm,
I think I like you
best:

Ever since the Big
Bang, ever since Genesis,
ever since the Milky Way gave birth
to a green-blue baby
called Earth—

All down the generations
of amorous plankton,
the dynasties of protozoa,
whole species that married and merged
into new species,
brewing up an atmosphere of
hospitable chemicals...

Down the golden ages
in the Garden, whole
civilizations of bacteria
that slowly grew into specialized
cells of one another,
building over millennia
the confederation of organs...

Ever since Evolution
conceived a tribe of naked mammals
begotten by the lineage
of Chimpanzee, I think
of all the protoplasm in the diaspora
of Creation, you
are my favorite animal

## This Side of the Glass

Not everyone is this lucky.
The mortgage is paid up.
The room is snug and warm.
The bed is comfortable,
and I'm not lying here
alone. Our new roof
keeps the weather outside
where it belongs,
where we can keep on eye on it
from any window.
The storm systems of human
cruelty and greed
stay on their side
of the glass, too, gone
at the click of the remote.
Yet every so often we wake up
on a morning just like this
to find that the cat
has brought in a headless
chipmunk or squirrel
to remind us
why we need this refuge,
or a live bird,
flapping frantically
from window to window,
to remind us
we are trapped here
and the wide-open world
of wild, free wind
and unbounded light
is beckoning
from the other side of the glass.

## Farewell, Blackbird Hotel

*The urge to climb a stump*
*must be a distant*
*forerunner of the itch*
*to mount a pulpit*
*or a throne . . .*

It's a call I can't resist.
No sooner do I turn around
and miss something huge and familiar
than I have to climb
the muddy steps to this mud lot
suddenly vacant, where
a dilapidated house no longer crumbles,
where my neighbor's magnificent
water oak stood
for some ninety years.

Standing on the monumental stump
in the fog of the streetlights
above the wet street
as a light drizzle comes down,
the rubble and debris around me shining
with a fresh snowfall
of sawdust, I look around
from a broad, high platform
of solid oak
sawn unevenly across the grain and see
my old house across the street
in new light.

Almost the same age,
the young house
taller at first but gradually eclipsed
as the trunk grew
and the branches spread, dozing
in its companionable shade for decades
of summers

before the longago winter when I
moved in, witnessing
the armada of blackbirds that arrived
every year
to fill those branches not so much
with song as with chatter,
like intermission at the opera,
like a blackbird hotel,
a leafy skyscraper towering
over my aging
rafters and shingles—

Over near one edge
of the ninety-some rings of longevity
exposed by the chainsaws,
two small hollow tunnels
lined with black rot
disappear into the massive roots.
The old tree still had years,
maybe another decade, but the end
had begun
and some days it definitely was
leaning my way.  Walking up
a truncated remnant
of the gigantic fallen trunk,
stepping down onto heavy round
cross-sections of oak,
I head back across the street,
across the rushing shadows
of almost a century,
toward the lighted windows of home.

*Next morning*
*even the stump was gone.*
*The workmen came back early*
*and woke the whole block*
*with the mournful wails of the saw,*
*the keening grinder . . .*

## For Lack of Evidence

The bug that died
in my drink—

Dried-up earthworms
that didn't make it across
the hot sidewalk—

A black cat beside the freeway
that tried to cross
the path of one too many
humans—

The skeletons of birds
that guide me
through this wilderness
of cracked cement—

The tiny perfect hands
of a dead rat, curled
around the same elusive
emptiness
I've tried to grasp all my life—

Cigarette butt,
gum wrapper, bottlecap
lying there serenely
unperturbed
by the contradictions of living—

All these clues
left behind
wherever I happen to look down
explain nothing
to the detectives, but
tell the whole story at a glance
to the witness.

*If this world is a mystery,*
*it's not*
*for lack of evidence.*

## The Naked Scientist

I am the naked scientist
singing as I set my specimens free
Joyfully I observe the positions of things
and nudge them off their courses,
gauge their direction and budge them
from their places

The green things around me lap my exhalations,
my fresh odors startle the ancient
solution of gases, I let my hand pass experimentally
down the mossy flank of a boulder
purring in the sun

I ache sometimes at sunrise
for the waking of the world to what it knows
Each day I gather data, and grieve
for the grieving of one or two or eleven people
I hadn't counted before

And I look over my notes at sunset
comforted by this work of the Study of Woe,
calculating my Theory of Revelation
in the face of entropy and decay

I live to know this world as my grandmother
knew her Bible, but best of all
I love the pilgrimage
of the search—

(Shall I tell you my discovery?
It is all alive.
And the snowflakes are not
all one sex.)

## Grandmother's Seeds

>   for Anna Maude, my grandmother

She's out in her garden,
bending down to touch the soil.
She covers each seed as she
must have tucked me into bed, long
ago.  Her old hoe is worn
to a shining crescent, sifting
earth into dark flour.

She never knew the shelves
in her bathroom were lined with
the signs of the zodiac.
I never heard her mention the moon.
She sprinkled poison like
holy water and thanked the Lord
for filling her deep-freeze.

She sits at the lamp
over her morning devotions.
Outside in the dimness
the first seed stirs in the ground.
She folds her glasses, closes
her book on its bookmark and goes out
to turn on the hose.

## Lost Leaf

### for Carol Ann, my mother

She'll never drive
out that road again, she says,
even to visit her old neighbors

The land might be different now,
new fruit trees, new
fences, but sleeping
in it everywhere are her hands

As if each thrust of the spade
in the garden took root, each beat
of her pulse pushed through
the dry stones in the creekbed
from a buried heart

Records in the county courthouse
save her signature like
a flattened October leaf
through the winters

But the land is the same
and her memories lie cramped
in the spring buds, waiting,
her hunger to be there
hums like the yellowjacket nest
under the rafters of the barn

## Native Blood

My Native American ancestors don't say much

When my DNA test results came back,
the Native generations that spawned me
didn't speak up

But I remember my grandmother telling me
she'd always wondered
about the dark face in that old family photo
in her parents' house
that sat on the piano and never
said a word

And in my grandfather's family cemetery,
off to one side
of a lively conversation
in cut and chiseled granite,
a circle of rough stones kneeling in the grass
says nothing

Meanwhile, the red clay of every stripped
and ravaged hill
runs down along the scars of erosion
in every rainstorm like rills
and runnels and rivulets of native blood

It doesn't matter whose DNA I carry around
as I walk or drive
these steep-pitched streets, this stolen homeland
of my inheritance, doesn't matter one bit
what percentage of who I am
came from where

The mud-red rivers rolling down between the hills
carry oxygen
to every cell in my body, murmuring the names
of ancestors we all share
in a language that will outlive us

The red-barked pines standing along every highway
in beds of damp red needles
silently keep watch

My Native American ancestors keep quiet
and stay out of sight

## Asphalt Nights

Looking back now, I often
regret that night in my delinquent youth
when I impulsively
borrowed a shovel and buried
my memories of childhood down by the creek
under a full moon.
How was I to know the entire floodplain
would be paved for parking
when they built the new mall?
Night after night now I dream I'm a lost child
roaming mile after mile
of fresh black asphalt under the floodlights
between the slumbering cars,
kicking my shadow ahead with every step,
stopping to listen
at every storm drain for the faint
trickle or drip of some other world
to wake up in.

## The Country I Love Has No Flag
### (Only Blossoms)

*It's a love that grows deeper*
*every Spring*
*when she perfumes herself with flowers*
*and lures me once more into the dance . . .*

He dreads flying over the Northwest now,
the airline pilot tells me
over vegetables and dip, looking down
on the acres of desolation hidden from the highway,
and remembers aloud for me
the story of Lindbergh, who hated flying
over the country he loved
while it bloomed with hard-working
little cancer cells, that homicidal mania
for cutting and building and paving
and selling off
and moving west again, so he retreated
to a virgin island in Hawaii—
far enough west, anyhow, for his broken old heart
to pretend he had outpaced
the long invasion—

The country I love is a loud, rude whore
compared to the green beauty
that opened her legs and ate the first invaders,
yards deep with decaying leaves
under tall, arching hardwoods
all the way to the Mississippi, thick
with towering grasses
across the plains to the Rockies,
a million-year accumulation of rich dark topsoil
where generation after generation
of would-be conquerors now
lie buried—

She has swallowed her fill of us now
and lies dying of indigestion
while we devour her from within, oilrigs
like eager piglets lined up at the motherfountain,
combines sucking greedily
till the deep aquifers go dry,
bulldozers rumbling off the assembly line
and up the ridges, burying enemy soldiers alive
as dutifully as they
push over stumps in the clearcut—

The country I love has no flag, only blossoms
multicolored and fragrant,
a hillside of wildflowers, a busful of faces,
wave after wave of invaders
still washing up with the oilslicks and the jellyfish,
falling for her cheap
neon charm all over again, years or decades
after first seeing her face on some
flickering screen
with subtitles in Urdu or Swahili or Malay—

Under cemeteries poisoned
with the graves of witch-burners and Klansmen
and Jew-haters like Lindbergh,
under subdivisions scarred
with red-lining and gerrymandering,
under schoolyards scabbed with fresh cement,
highwaysides tattooed with the obscene
graffiti of billboards,
under the brownfields and the slums,
the golf courses and parking decks,
under the airport slab and the stockyards
lies the real country I love—

*It's a love that must go*
*unconsummated, alas, since this democracy*
*of do-gooders*
*has outlawed naked burial in the dirt . . .*

## Ten Years Eaten by the World

### for Blair Harman

Class reunion, cracked like the old bell
with an absence—
his tennis racket in my attic, his books,
his dusty typewriter...
I inherit not only the boxes of dead authors,
his fading blue
scrawl in the flyleaf, but the empty rocker
of his old age.

But the leisure for rocking and reading is
his alone, we flock
together for our reunion stung and grieving
our old freedom:
ten years out on our own in that world we still
call the real one,
world that buried him and so many from our
harvest of affluence—

*World that dumps its offal into rubber-lined pits*
*in the unacknowledged*
*earth, forgetting that what you plant there*
*grows back...*
*world that tombs its casualties in steel sarcophagi*
*so they won't turn*
*to fertilizer, forgetting that the earth eats*
*everything in the end...*

Passing all the strange young faces on these
familiar sidewalks,
I have to step out across the grassy carpet of the quad
to root myself again
in the dark world beneath all my goings: world
our cafeteria-gourmet
reunion dinner grew from while we saved and scrounged
our thirty bucks—

*World that pulses with the dark life of the soil,*
*eating and digesting,*
*world that terrorized the deathbeds of believers*
*and unbelievers alike . . .*
*birth-den of another pollinating spring,*
*world our young ones*
*still mistake for the real one till we get them*
*educated . . .*

As I do myself in my daydream on the Indian mound,
each of us adrift
in our solitary memories till the electric bell
chimes in the tower,
time for class, and we all jump, forgetting—

*We only walk the surface of what's real, don't we,*
*till we go where he's gone*

## A Glance Before Drinking

The water in the glass is deep and clear.
Particles of morning traffic
are dissolving there.
Slats of morning sun
afloat on its glittering, swaying surface
bounce up against the ceiling.
Lifting it to my lips for a drink
I am looking through the water,
through the glass,
tasting the spring where the daybreak swells
out of the earth.

## River Blues

The river
has gathered all the melancholy
of the rains— along with
mercury, sulphuric acid, coal particulates
rinsed out of the sky—
from ridgecrest to ridgecrest
a thousand braided streamlets come together
to bear that weight,
that audible accumulation
of silences

The river was once the center, now
it's a boundary:
gnawing patiently at the foundation of every
bridge that joins its banks,
hauling in a harvest of rich grains
of topsoil— mingled with
nitrogen, selenium, organophosphates
from the fields along its floodplain—
each farmer's private grief
suspended in its current as it glides
seaward

The river continues tirelessly
to arrive,
its million moving tons
threading dark as blood through the delta,
weaving marshes that teem
with amphibious lives,
depositing the silt and heartache of a continent
in a fertile, toxic debris
before dissolving into the fathomless
compassion of salt water...

*Wait a little, the last of it is not here yet,*
*every snake drags a tail*
*and no song goes on forever,*
*except maybe— wait a little*
*longer yet—*
*maybe the blues*

### Man Breathing Life into Metal

The saxophonist wets his lips
and caresses his mouthpiece

sucks it in and lets it escape
and then draws it back

into himself so its dark twisting
entrails join with his own

clamps the dormant light of that
gleaming muscle in his

fingertips and forces through its
thin lips from his own

the infinite compression of a breath:
the golden bell sings out

with the panic of inarticulate matter
waking to the agony it is

to be an animal, the joy it is
to move and speak and sing

> "*Now when I get through playing it,*
> *it going to be just as warm as my body . . .*"

## Moth

I bit my fingernails too short
waiting for this bus, I stood
too close to the road too long, peering
through the haze of engine fumes—

Everyone around me pretends not to know.
So naturally by now they've all
long since forgotten.
No one on this bus remembers
poetry overhead among the ads: today
hundreds of cockroach silhouettes,
the extermination campaign . . .

A dead moth
on the stairs in the train station knows:
startled black and red and yellow eyes
on shattered wings
stare past me through the concrete overhang,
and suddenly I see
right through the step I'm about to take—

Its furry underbody
leaves a yellow pollen on my fingertips.
Ridiculous
to carry the fallen creature home.
Ridiculous to choose one place
out of all the galaxies
to go.

## Microtrash

Microtrash:
anything smaller than a cigarette butt
made for human hands
by a machine,
dropped or tossed or otherwise
abandoned
to litter the sidewalk,
the roadside, the highway shoulder,
the trail
over a mountain pass
through legally designated
wilderness...

Microtrash—
any minute hint or trace or clue
no matter how small
that betrays the passing
of a two-legged beast with fingers
and a brain
riddled with tunnels
of deadly amnesia, convoluted
with a thousand channels of instant
nostalgia, flooded
with artificial light
and the chemical sugars
of loneliness...

Microtrash.
Bending down to pick it up
is the closest I ever come
to prayer.

## Lord of the Intersection

I glanced up
past the traffic light
as I sat waiting
and spotted him up there
surveying his busy
crowded domain
from his lookout post
at the top of the light pole
regal and alert
and perfectly at home
against the sky
and whatever he was
doing up there it was
the absolute
opposite of waiting—

Months later
parking the car
the moment I
swung open my door
a rocket with wings
shot by at knee-level
ascending gracefully
and as it cleared
the dead-end sign
on the corner
I finally registered
the silhouette of hawk
and dangling squirrel
and saw why
watching is
the opposite of waiting

## Where You Fell

The hooked beak
of a predator,
                    down
beside the phone booth

as I hung up on the busy signal

your neck rolling luxuriously
        back
as I bent to cradle you up

your wings still limber,
        fanning out
in a grey-brown brocade

your talons clamped on
        nothing
that could hold you

        your spirit flown

I take just one
of your chest-feathers,
brother,
        to remind me

hunter of these rainy streets

The rest of you I bury
        in the back yard
six blocks from where you fell

## Hawk in the Warehouse

Sitting here by the pond
surrounded by autumn gold
and green
beneath the open sky, I glance up
just in time to catch
a flash of birdflight
splitting the blue air
maybe six feet above my head,
and suddenly
                see
the sweep of wings
across a warehouse ceiling
forty feet up,
the long glide from rafter to rafter,
talons reaching
as the wings beat, braking,
to seize a diagonal steel strut
that braces
a corrugated sheet-metal sky—

She soars on soundless feathers
from corner to corner,
hunting for daylight
in the cold glare of fifty-odd
fluorescent bulbs.
She doesn't know
she's the emissary of a haunted
imagination, ghost of an ancient forest
long since sacrificed
for streets and parking lots
and warehouses.

But she knows
                that scent
drifting up from everything in this
breathless, windowless space,
knows enough
to launch herself again
across the dim starless ceiling
when I edge too close,
gazing up
awed and helpless—

*It's the odor of death.*
*Death for her and her babies.*
*Death for trees and sky.*
*Death for everything she loves*
*with her wide blue windy heart.*

An open door is an open door.
It's freedom. Ask anyone
who's ever been locked in a cage.
But the light
                framed
in each rectangular gap
along the loading dock
shows her nothing she knows.

She's getting hungry now.
But while this warehouse echoes
with human sounds,
she hides.
                She waits.

## Praising the Rain

I hear it coming
a minute or two before it arrives,
like stampeding buffalo
off in the distance, heading my way
from some long-vanished
Ghost Dance prairie
as I sit concentrating, distracted,
here on my screened-in
back porch—
and then suddenly
it's here, shaking the ground
like the pounding hoofbeats
of a herd of caribou
migrating through my quiet
neighborhood, thundering across
the Arctic tundra of my roof,
invisible in the dustcloud
of mist and humidity they raise
behind them—
like an explosion of small
flashing wings, a whirlwind swarm
of Old Testament locusts
devouring every blade and leaf
of thought or memory in my head
for a brief and endless
roaring, howling, trance-like
span of time—
and then just as suddenly
it's gone, I hear it galloping on
to the next neighborhood, and then
those same three musical
notes again—

All through the peak
of the downpour,
that three-note birdcall never stopped
praising the rain

## Visitors from the Sky

The geese
stand around on the wet puddled
pavement
in the parking lot, one
balanced on just one
leg, a lost flock
loitering here as I cut
through
to avoid the traffic light at the corner

Fashionably dressed
season after season, they look around
quietly
unconscious of their classic looks—
long black sinuous necks,
plump tawny bodies,
stylish white chinstrap just
behind the eyes—
unaware
of the pride in their bearing,
the absolute confidence of the wild,
completely ignorant
that they are even Canada geese—

Every year they touch down precisely
here
to wander the wide flat asphalt,
the shorn grass that stretches
to the curb,
the street itself
in casual twos and threes
and informal clusters, like tourists
disembarking from the bus
to stretch
and smoke and pose for snapshots

As if once upon a time a lake
or a marsh
beckoned here
amid the endless miles of treetops,
and generation after generation
of mystified wild geese
still arrive, spring after spring,
fall after fall
expecting water,
a rest stop on the great
annual migration
since long before humans were human

Or perhaps they drift
afloat
in exactly that spontaneous
formation
on some parallel planet
where water still covers its old haunts
with acres of jeweled wavelets
and blue mirrors of sky,
world where I'm
just a phantom intruder
staring
from the window of my car—

After I've gazed a while
they begin to grow
self-conscious,
shifting their positions
one by one
until the whole flock is sidling along
not yet alarmed but clearly
wary,
unsure of my intentions

And for a second I'm not so sure
myself:
late for work, as usual,
grateful for this dumbstruck vision
of the naked universe,
wondering if these illustrious travelers
are simply lost, or if it's this
human carnival
of lights and rides, gaudy prizes
and cotton candy,
barkers and pickpockets and shills
that's lost its path
among the stars instead

I watch
until the one-legged traveler
unfurls his missing foot
and we all
ease into motion again,
going our opposite
but eternally converging
ways

*See you in six months, elegant friends.*
*Eat well. Stay together.*
*Travel safe.*

## The Earth Forgives Everyone in the End

### 1.

Ignore the whine of cars
out on the highway.
That's only temporary.
Here in the trees the wind tells us
all we need to know.
The microscopic hairs of roots
bring us everything we need
to live. Rotting leaves
speak softly underfoot and need
no translation. The Earth
forgives everyone in the end.

### 2.

Trash in the recycling,
        recyclables
in the trash

The ocean gives a little,
        takes a little
back

Even the grownups
        will eventually grow up
and get it

The Earth forgives
        everyone
in the end

3.

*When I am finally lowered into*
    *a hole,*
*the elaborately constructed*
    *illusion*
*that I am somehow separate from*
    *the soil*
*will gradually*
    *disintegrate*

*The Earth forgives everyone*
    *in the end*


## Marginalia

A tiny black bug skitters
along the edge
of my book.
My eyes stray from the page.
My thoughts veer off
on the shiny steel rail that leads
efficiently, judiciously,
to premeditated murder.
My eyes follow the bug instead.
At the corner
where the cut edge of the paper
turns, he flexes
tiny wings. He hesitates. I bend
to blow him gently off
into the air. He's
a part of this household, too,
right?

## Daylight Calling

The young rooster's first attempt to crow
is squeaky and uncertain,
a shaky, unmusical phrase.

But as the days go by his confidence grows—
confidence in himself or faith
in the morning, I'm not sure which—
until after a month of steady practice
he bellows that age-old salute to the new,
the original reveille,
in a rendition absolutely his own.

We named our first rooster Blossom:
a fryer, maybe a broiler,
who somehow fell off a truck
and showed up in our back yard one day.
It was months before the telltale
spurs on his heels, the splendid red comb
and majestic wattles
gave his true gender away.

Bred to grow fat
in a cage and die at a tender age,
Blossom announced every sunrise for three years
until at last his heart
could no longer haul his weight around.
The morning after we buried him,
his number-one hen hopped up to perch
on a weathered segment of log
and uttered a long, brokenhearted croak
of a crow.

Stretched out here comfortably in the dark,
in no way ready for daylight,
I recognize that arrogant trumpet.
It's the call of duty, a triumphant reminder
that every one of us is here for a reason.
One more opportunity to live it out,
or at least to persevere in the search for it,
is about to sear the horizon.

Refusing to wake up is no longer an option.


## The Stones Cry Out

Ours is not the only intelligence.
The stones too cry out
with the glory of sunrise.
A crooked pine towers over every truth.

The chipmunk whirls and is gone
before its small striped
electrical impulse reaches my brain.
Mushrooms last a little longer.
The moss remains.

The distant clamor of last night's news
barely ripples the loon's inscrutable
reflection. Rosebud,
grasshopper, translucent moon...

Even this stained concrete,
now that I stoop to admire
the embedded speckle of gravel
from some gutted riverbank—

The stones cry out.
The moss remains.

## Grasshopper Man, Driving Through
### for Gary Snyder

*I live on a planet,*
the rising moon
reminds me,
huge and round and low
above the wires
and rooftops of the city

*I live in a watershed,*
brown water reminds me,
slow and quiet
and powerful,
curving through trees,
reflecting sky
as I cross the interstate bridge

*I belong to an ancient
mountain range,*
the first unmistakable
distant blue
shape of a mountain
reminds me
as I round a curve
on the highway north

*I am one cell
of an unimaginably immense
multicellular creature,*
sunlight
glinting from the bright green
multitudes of spring
reminds me
as I pass between two
towering mountainsides

*Just one small part
of something grand . . .
Does that make me small
or grand?*

## The Writer on His Bicycle

Dressed in his regular
everyday clothes,
stylish helmet strapped to his chin
especially for this poem,
he rides gleefully aware of his influence
over generations to come
who will look back amazed
that in those distant times
of upheaval, when a lazy
ignorant nation confronted its own
blank face in the blank screen
of yet another power outage,
amid that age of epidemic
insanity a few had faith
enough to swing one leg
over, catch the pedals and chase
one sneaker with the other
like a vast, infinitely complex planet
going nowhere
but around

On some hill of despair
the bonfire
you kindle can light the great sky—
though it's true, of course, to make it burn
you have to throw yourself in . . .

> *Galway Kinnell*
> *"Another Night in the Ruins"*

# (3)
# Hurtling Through Darkness

## House of the Sky

### 1.

Once I'm irrevocably committed,
crawling bumper to bumper
up the freeway ramp, I lean
to my glovebox
to check the map—

                Yes,
the right road

                    *Yes,*
*mutters the raccoon*
*curled up in its striped tail*
*on the shoulder of the interstate*

The road to the mountains
is jammed with commuters,
each headed home
to a wired and insulated burrow
while I inch along
                    among them
toward the house of the sky

One by one the other cars disappear
down side roads and driveways,
gradually the trees begin to outnumber
the utility poles—

                    *This way,*
*murmurs the pointed snout of a possum*
*face-down beside the highway*

(The trees stand
along the mountain curves
ready to catch me
                    and teach me
in one quick lesson
whatever my species still doesn't get
about assaulting nature
head-on)

## 2.

Bless this stony ground I
stumble over,
following the steel blade
of the road grader
around the edge of a steep, dry hollow
on my slow descent
       into the quiet
carrying my backpack and tent

*Roof of naked branches,*
*rug of damp golden leaves*
*deep-piled*
     *wall to wall*
*Windows of rain and light and cloud*
*framed in second-growth*
*hardwood*

The campfire is good company,
purring like a mountain lion too well fed
to be dangerous
     as I toss it
another forked antler of pine

*Welcome, stranger*
     *it growls*

Swinging in my hammock
between two trees,
     I muse
across the meadow
into a scrawny remnant of the great
North American temperate forest

*Welcome, child*
     *it whispers*

(Strange
   and fitting
to arrive in this peaceful house
strapped safe in the engine
that is blindly, busily
burning it down)

## The Deer That Flew

The deer that flew across my windshield
in the last second of her life,
what was she telling me?

The doe that bounded suddenly out of the dark
into my headlights like a vision
or a hallucination
must have been traveling almost as fast as I was
on a perpendicular course, direct
as a bullet:
and sooner or later, perpendiculars meet.

She came from another world.
She didn't see my little car
or the semi-truck we were passing,
the long flat wall of trailer towering on our right,
never saw the glaring beams,
heard the stampeding whine of the Interstate . . .

Or perhaps— ancient superstition never quite
discredited by science—
she simply had no other way of getting my
attention.
Her message from that quiet world
of woods and streams and starlight
was too urgent.
She planted her rear right hoof on the pavement
where our trajectories crossed,
and it was too late to turn my wheel.

She never said a word.
She twisted my fender with her delicate haunch
and vanished, leaving only
the shudder of impact, a shimmy
in my right front wheel,
a shattered headlight assembly
to instruct me.

I knew she was already gone, down, dead,
instantly in another world
altogether.
But in the wake of silence
behind our engine-noise and passenger-talk,
she still soars
over the shadowy abyss
between me and that speeding eighteen-wheeler...

Perpendicular to this world, another lies hidden.
My headlight shines aimlessly up
as if pointing the way.

### Dry Season

Sitting on a boulder
left behind
amid the silt and scattered leaves
of a dry streambed
where the long-gone tumble and rush
of current
laid bare the roots of trees
and carved out a channel
between overhanging banks,
gazing downstream
toward the puddled seeping creek,
the high-banked river,
the steadily rising ocean,
while the afternoon drains away
into twilight,
I send a prayer out
to the gods of drought and ruin
for the rain's return.

## Bundle of Bones

At first, flashing past
in the fast lane, I thought I saw
a sack of trash, tossed
or bounced
from the bed of some passing pickup.
Then, in the instant
it disappeared, I glanced down.
Dead coyote, trapped
between the asphalt shoulder
and the concrete median wall,
surrounded
by the unforgiving city— pelt
bleached ghost-white,
skin drawn tight, bones protruding
like the random contents
of one more
anonymous sack of trash
beside the freeway—
Dead coyote, slowly shrinking
into an effigy of itself,
melting into sunlight and air, vanishing
little by little through pavement
into the dank, dark earth
from which it sprang,
already running,
on the very first day.
Not a vision. Just a glimpse
of incorruptible faith,
a sacred bundle of bones
I carry with me
still.

## Effortlessly Uphill

Smoothly,
eagerly,
effortlessly the car
climbs the hill
under the casual pressure of my foot.
The quiet whisper under the hood
swells to a murmur,
the scenery tilts a few degrees
upward around me.
When I crest the rise I barely notice
I am easing back
on the accelerator pedal
as the pavement gradually
levels off
under my tires.

A hundred years ago
a team of horses
strains against the traces
of a wagon stacked with firewood, grunting
in their leather harness,
puffing steam into the winter afternoon,
burning oats and hay
to produce a glistening froth
of sweat and effort,
hauling their cargo up a steep road
paved with dried mud
in braided ruts
between new-built bungalows
where an asphalt street will someday
climb between
these same granite curbstones ...

Two hundred years ago
a man with skin as black
as his shadow
bends nearly double from the waist,
a fifty-pound sack of field corn
across one shoulder,
powered by salted beans and cornbread,
his naked torso glazed
with dust and perspiration, wiping
salt water from his eyebrows
with his free hand and slinging it away
with a gesture of rebuke,
breathing out
a husky curse with every exhalation,
cussing his way up that same
steep unpaved road
through a hillside pasture . . .

Three hundred years ago
a merry cluster of women and girls
with nut-brown faces
carrying baskets of chestnuts gathered
over a long morning
of gossip and laughter
follows a duff-cushioned path
as it begins to ascend
between flowering dogwoods
and colonnades of oak
in green-tinted shade and stippled sunlight,
chewing dried venison
to fuel the long walk home,
lapsing into silence as they work their way
in breathless zigzag steps
up the long incline
of that very same hill.

Far across the foothills
and the coastal plain,
beyond the curvature of horizon,
somewhere out at sea
a tanker churns through whitecaps
headed for the docks
of Newport, burning the dirtiest
byproduct of petroleum
to push its load of crude oil from Dubai
toward the pipeline
and the refinery, the tanker truck
and the gas station,
finally my fuel injection system
to haul my plush seat
serenely up this hill I barely
even notice
I am climbing.

## Distant Singing

Listen:
somewhere off in the distance,
a motor.
It too has a song.
It's the song of pushing eagerly forward,
heedless of how,
careless of where,
regardless of why,
intoxicated
with the singleminded joy
of burning its little tank of fuel,
never mind
where the fuel came from
or where that little plume of smoke
might go.

## The Graveyard of Empires

Counting up the numbers
on the even-numbered side of the road,
looking for a post office rumored
open on Saturdays,
I glance across the street and suddenly I'm
counting back the years
of a cemetery

All this horsepower and commotion
just to arrive at the next
red light
a little faster than the rest

> *Instant Credit*
> *for Bankruptcy*
> *Bad Credit*
> *Single Married*
> *or Divorced*
> *Walk In Ride Out*

From our beautiful machines
we watch the trees come down, the hills
scraped level and sealed under
an impervious façade
of asphalt and glass and concrete
lit up at frequent intervals with bright
cheerful ads

Our gleaming fenders
so immaculately waxed that we don't dare
touch, trusting one another
mightily
to stay in our lanes

While the deserts spread
and the glaciers retreat, topsoil drifting
away on the wind, dead zones
metastasizing offshore
where the rivers spill into the seas...

Even me, with my low-flush toilet
and high-mileage car,
I can't claim ignorance, much less
plead innocent: I too
own a share in this destruction,
it pays me interest each day,
each minute,
deposited in my secret account
at the funeral parlor

But in the hour close to sunset,
as I head home
and the manhole covers turn
to burning coins in the pavement,
electrical emanations
shining off the smog, twilight
seeping in like a sorrowful tide,
I know
how tentative it all is

Because all roads lead
sooner or later to the edge
of civilization
where a barren, smoky wasteland
begins...

> *Mama, did you know that once*
> *long ago*
> *they had stores that sold nothing*
> *but convenience?*

## Inscription Found Among the Ruins

Convenience is my god, I shall not wait!
He maketh me lunch to go at the drivethru window;
he leadeth me with canned laughter;
he replenisheth my cash.
He delivereth from the sweatshops of Asia
        my name-brand in a plastic sack.
Yeah, though I cruise the freeways of the metropolis of death,
I will see and hear and smell no evil,
for gas is cheap.
My satellite dish and my remote they pacify me.
Thou preparest a tray for me in a pressurized eggshell
        high in the air;
thou anointest my head with mousse gel;
my cup is one hundred percent disposable.
Surely dumpsters and landfills will swallow my
        throwaway days
and I will bask in the microwaves of my own convenience
happily ever after.
                Amen!

## Washed in the Hurricane

High above this quiet place
under the trees,
the roar of one jet after another
rises and subsides like the restless surf
of an ocean
fouled with floating petroleum, each flight
just beginning to fade as the next
surges over
while I sit surrounded
by an invisible cloud of testifying
crickets—

*You can deny it to yourself
in every bubble
of carbon dioxide you exhale,* they chorus
in their ancient counterpoint
and harmony. *But we can't pretend
this is the same world
our ancestors shared with yours
since the beginning. Did you forget?
How long did you imagine
you could go on pumping out the fumes
of a billion tailpipes and smokestacks
without altering
the chemical composition
of the sky?*

Stealthy and slow,
lapping up another inch of beachfront,
the sea level rises steadily
through the night.
High tide washes through the streets
of Miami. London
barricades the banks of the Thames.

Island nations from the Maldives
to the Marshalls
prepare to surrender
their sovereign homelands
to the sea.

Meanwhile, somewhere
out on the Atlantic,
air currents swirl
counterclockwise, drawing salt water up
into turbulent vapor as they pass
over the warm waves,
spiraling inward toward a center
of inexplicable stillness, a single eye
in the brow of the storm
surrounded by stampeding circular winds
spanning five hundred miles, spinning
two hundred miles an hour,
twisting and whipping
in unpredictable directions until it
predictably
intersects a vulnerable stretch of coastline
where the protective shield
of wetlands has been replaced
with beachfront condominums.  Now
as the sea warms and fresh water
dilutes the salt,
any tropical cyclone can turn
into the rampaging one-eyed monster
the ancient Greeks
named "Cyclops"
and the Weather Channel simply calls
"Category Five."

Melting under the winter sun,
the glaciers of Norway
and Iceland and Tibet
shrink into postcards of themselves.
Tourists stand in line
at Glacier National Park
to see them before they're gone.
Massive islands of ice break free
from the Antarctic ice sheet
like renegade whales
abandoning their families to travel on
alone. Starving polar bears
float away on orphaned floes, lost
among the icebergs
of the Arctic Sea.

So what if a hostile foreign power
launched a surprise attack
tomorrow at sunrise,
and our leaders answered only
with excuses and lies,
more excuses and more lies,
because they all had lucrative
private investments
in enemy shipyards and munitions plants?
*Climate! That's just
a fancy word for weather.
The weather is always changing anyway.
A hurricane making landfall
is good for the economy!
Even the laws of physics can be overturned
by a friendly judge.
And no international agreement
will stand up in court
if it unfairly burdens those
who've grown rich
laying waste to the Earth.
Just read the fine print!*

Like a vengeful army
of suicide bombers, wildfires
ravage the Texas panhandle,
overrun British Columbia and Oregon,
overwhelm the brave defenders
of southern California,
storming ridge after ridge,
swallowing whole towns
and spitting out cinders.
New Zealand and Australia,
France and Portugul battle their own
blazing insurgencies.
No one understands
why the woods and fields
are so angry.

Meanwhile, a many-colored serpent
eight lanes wide
crawls in sinuous curves
across the land, each glittering scale
dreaming it's the star
of its own TV commercial, a fantasy
of freedom and conquest,
speed and precision and grace.
From sea to shining sea, the oil rigs
and pipelines and refineries
quietly spew their petrochemical poison
into the water
that human bone-marrow uses
to make blood.
Burnt hydrocarbons ascend
into the heavens
like a demonic host. Asthmatic children
struggle for one more breath.
And every year is hotter
than the year before.

*Everyone in the world knows*
*it is the Manifest Destiny*
*of every American*
*to freely burn the Earth's reserves*
*of oil, coal, and gas*
*blowing leaves off the lawn*
*and lighting up every inch of the night.*
*The freedom we fought for*
*in war after war turns out to be*
*the all-too-human right*
*to use up and throw away*
*our only world, one plastic spoon*
*and styrofoam cup at a time.*
*And everyone*
*in the world*
*wants to be an American.*

Drought
magnifies the sun
burning over Central America,
Sub-Saharan Africa,
the Middle East, baking the soil
to a crust of rock and dust.
Drought drives the farmers
from their dying fields and orchards
to the cities, feeding the flames
of famine and frustration.
Refugees clog the roads
going anyplace that will take them,
a procession of sanctuary-seekers
that stretches indefinitely
into the future.

But there is no asylum
on a warming planet.
The atmosphere grows steadily
less stable, more volatile,
like molecules of water in a pot
about to boil:
a little nervous at first, gradually
aggravated, finally frantic, ricocheting
from extreme to extreme.
Record-breaking snowstorms
pile confusion on top of
disinformation on top of ignorance
on top of denial, all of it resting
on a firm foundation of habit
dug, reinforced, poured and hardened
in the sandy soil
of human arrogance.

*You can tune in*
*the news channel of your choice,*
the crickets chant
from their primeval temples
in the underbrush.
*You can memorize and regurgitate*
*all the slogans and jingles,*
*soundbites and scriptures,*
*affirmations and incantations it takes*
*to persuade yourself*
*you live all alone in a world*
*you invented. We'll keep on patiently*
*reminding you.*
*We don't live in your world.*
*You have always*
*lived in ours.*

## The Enemy Logo

The gas station signs glow
above the treetops along the highway,
brighter than the moon,
eclipsing the sun, gleefully mocking
our desperate addiction to anything
that burns...

*History? Suicidal hijackers
in the cockpit of the nation.
A ship with its rudder welded to the keel.
Decent, honest citizens
serving a machine
that's programmed to devour them
just as soon as it gets
cheaper than feeding them.*

We've been bombing ourselves
with nuclear waste
for decades now, cooking the atmosphere
for centuries, breathing airborne
particles of incinerated old-growth,
greedily burning everything
we can steal...

*Progress? A child playing
on a precipice.
A vast, proud, imperial civilization
mistaking a way of life
for life itself.
The most luxurious palaces that ever
collapsed into a rabid surf.*

Finally we have no choice but to begin
burning the furniture, setting fire
to heaps of plastic toys
and synthetic clothing, the flames
giving off just enough light to see
this darkness, if we only dared
to open our eyes...

## The Dividends of Sin

A baby gazes up
from its stroller, just ahead of me
in the checkout line:
dark eyes so steady, so direct,
that after a minute
that goes on and on I have to glance
around
for any excuse
to look someplace else.

But everywhere my eyes try
to rest, they see only
evidence
of another crime.

Everywhere the innocent are
going down,
species by species
disappearing
into the spreadsheets of taxonomists,
the window displays
of taxidermists, the footnotes
of children's textbooks.

And everywhere the children
are abandoning their classrooms
for the capitol steps,
picking up microphones
to chant in unison the things
their parents are ashamed to remember,
too busy running
the machinery of progress
to hear.

And inside the capitol,
the testimony of scientists weighs nothing
against the stock value
of the multinational syndicates
of organized crime,
those cartels
that bank their future revenues
in underground deposits of disaster
and deprivation.

And far away, across
the rising seas,
another dark-eyed child wakes up hungry,
bathed in precious water
from the tear-ducts of a farmer
whose harvest lies
parched and shriveling
in the heat
of another season of drought.

My pizza is ready.
The young family with the stroller
has already paid and gone.
I step up to the register to pay my share
of the rising cost
of complicity— the kingpin's bonus,
the triggerman's *per diem*—
open my box and bite
into my stockholder's dividend.

## Understood

Yes,
our grandchildren will curse us.
Granted.
But they will never understand how absolutely
necessary it was
to just get in the car and go.
How unthinkable it was to just sit
still, waiting
for the Grand Canyon to come
to us, for the empty ketchup bottle to run
to the store
and replenish itself. For so long, *to go*
was simply a synonym for
*to live.* The world was waiting here
for all those evolutionary ages clearly just
for us. Why else
would it be so irresistibly
flammable?

Our grandchildren will curse us.
Understandable.
But they will never have to decide which evil
is the lesser,
to relinquish all control
over steering and accelerator and brakes
on the subway or the bus,
or to imagine
an imperceptibly slow, immeasurably vast,
inconceivably far-reaching catastrophe
in an improbable future
which might be foreclosed anyway

any second now
by incoming missiles, if not
a simple heart attack
or highway accident. And now
that they will never have
the luxuries they accuse us of refusing
to give up,
how will they ever know how seductive it was
to shovel the future of the world
into the furnace
and watch it burn?

For generations, for millennia,
children dutifully revered their elders.
But that was in some
other world
which we hereby bequeath to all the generations
of posterity, preserved
in a million movies and TV shows,
vintage commercials,
landfills and junkyards. But irretrievably
gone. Yes, our grandchildren will curse us.
Understood.
But still. Just one more trip
to the mall, one more Caribbean
vacation...

## Hurtling Through Darkness

Hurtling
between the silver ribbons
uncurling eternally
out through the darkness,
steering by a chain of diamonds
strung through space,

I start again every time
I stray from my lane and they
bump under my tires, the reflecting
eyes of all the animals
who have died for this highway—

Focusing my own wild eyes
into the rainstorm,
the floodlights of billboards,
the pulse of blue lightning
at the power plant,

leaning back in the cushioned engine
of my will
with the road's vibration
humming in my vitals,
gripping the steering wheel as tight as my life,

I ride the thirsty beast
of my momentum, obedient to the signs,
barely in control,
hurtling through the darkness of the eons
of extinction

## Carcasses Rusting in a Field

It's quiet here in the junkyard.
Mud roads bump through acres of dead grass
        and the plundered wrecks of automobiles.
The grass waits to wake again in the spring.
The wrecks wait for reincarnation,
        horn by fender, manifold by windowglass.
They remind me of the rusting casualties of some war
        parked in long rows up and down the pasture,
        chewing over their deformities and defeats.
In the distance I hear the highway,
        booming voices of those who imagine
        the roads run on forever.
But here in the junkyard it's quiet.

*We found your body abandoned*
        *by the side of the road.*
*You can rest here till you remember*
        *where you came from,*
        *all your alloys and polymers,*
        *and return there.*
*Take your time.*
*There is no hurry.*

## Spirals of Fire

*Once we have begun to fear the sky,*
*what can shelter us?*

We fill the air with the noise and exhaust
of our toxic distractions
and suicidal
accomplishments—
a conflagration of scorching drought
and melting icecaps,
the charred lungs of the jungle,
a world of intricate perfection
burning down
to a bed of coals—

*So who are we to label that humble weed*
*an invasive species?*

In case you hadn't noticed,
this everyday universe
is one vast miracle, woven of innumerable
tiny ones—
cellular, microbial, subatomic—
and even those unthinkably huge ones
we call galaxies,
nebulae, supernovae,
are infinitely small in comparison
to the whole—

*And I can pretend I own this tree*
*that's older than I am?*

Meanwhile the Earth
spirals on
around the galaxy, delivering a message
in a code called DNA—
a spiral, in case you didn't know,
is a circle
that's going somewhere, a spin
plus a direction,
and everything you see is constructed
of interlocking spirals—

*Do the digits on your clock*
*have a destination someplace?*

The night that seems to surround us,
in case you've forgotten,
is actually a dark expanse
deep in the heart
where the little sparkling lives of certain
thoughts
spread a subtle brilliance
to the edges and corners of the body
whose cells we are—

*Can you feel the hunger of the flames,*
*this oxygen-starved life?*

Kick the coals
apart, and suddenly your fire
is not a fire any more
but a constellation of embers
pulsing faintly with the recollection
of what fire was,
fading
quietly into ash . . .

*Plant something that will tower over you*
*someday!*

## Because We Believe

Because we believe it,
it's true.  Yes, once
upon a time in fact the world was
absolutely flat
for a millennium or so . . .

*Through a crack in the street*
*an old trolley rail peeks through*
*from another world*
*hidden under the asphalt, a lost age*
*filled with ordinary days*
*like ours*

Because they
believe it, it's true.
The future is a frightening place
and we're all
on our way there right now.

*Maybe the lemmings*
*aren't so suicidal after all*
*Maybe they just keep*
*following the wrong leaders*

Faith is simply the will to trust
that doing right is good
and vice versa, and virtue
is its own
humanitarian award.
Because you believe it,
it's true.

*Earth Day's come and gone again,*
*and all that's left*
*is this box of Earth Day posters*
*it's my job to recycle*
*and the incandescent curve*
*of another dawn*

Like those diehards who cheerfully,
nonchalantly recycle
every scrap, pedal to work
and refuse to buy plastic
as if some kind
of future was actually
possible—

*These hugs, are they*
*part of the dance?*
*Does the cool mountain stream*
*still cost nothing to drink?*
*Can I hold on to these good friends*
*as long as the world goes on*
*breathing around me?*

You keep
the spoils of success,
as much as
you can carry
as you board your private jet
or rocketship
on your way out of town.
I'll take
the inhabited world,
its slow tides of sun
and shadow,
rainfall and transpiration,
this whirling
spectrum of energies
called Earth.

*I mean if love*
*is just a theory, well*
*what are we all here for anyway*
*if not to choose*
*some wild hypothesis*
*and test it?*

Because I believe it,
it's true.

## Pushing the Peace Bus

Pushing the Peace Bus was hardest
on the third try— feeling a little
like the old bus as we stumbled,
choking on its unsuccessful smoke,
never quite catching
the necessary breath,
the houses on the old street
hardly noticing...

Spent, sprawled,
winded and panting, pretty soon
we began to feel
the trees: a still surrounding
presence, arch of limbs
from both sides of the street
commingling above us, leafy
memory of woods to the horizon
as we rested, looking up, their roots
a living tangle in the dark beneath us—

We gave the fourth try everything we had:
one block from the dead-end sign,
the black arrow pointing us
east or west, we bent
to the bumper, leaning
clear to the pavement, our feet
a living tangle, muscles moving
somehow together—

Ten cases of slightly
bruised organic apples
on the roof, the rice and lentils,
firewood, pots and pans, big
jugs of water, all of it somehow
moving together, faster
till the clutch popped and smoke
backfired in our faces again
and the Peace Bus was chugging
once more over the fallen shadows
of branches, through the temples of sun...

We caught up at the stop sign and
climbed aboard. The Bus
turned the corner, choosing west,
leaving a pledge and prayer
to the trees in its drifting and
dissolving smoke.


## Daybreak at Eleven

Slow pump
        empty tank
                clear sky
Daybreak at eleven
        again

Smoky fire
        damp wood
                clouded moon
Another midnight
        supper

## Wildlife Opening

We have camped in this wildlife opening
for a hundred thousand years,
since human beings were only one more twig
on a single branch
of the vast living wilderness,
before we learned the art of clearing trees
with fire, making openings
for crops to grow, for astronomers
to gaze out at the stars

We return to camp once more
in this meadow cleared to lure the deer
within range of the hunter's gun
in this time when all the arts of fire
are burning out of control,
changing the very chemistry of the air
all creatures breathe,
an entire civilization hurtling
at the speed of electricity
down a dead-end highway

We come together in this forest clearing
to learn the art of growing wild again,
to listen to these trees
instructing us with their deep-searching roots
how to anchor ourselves in the Earth,
describing with their reaching limbs
how to embrace the sky,
repeating over and over
in every blossoming bud and fallen leaf
how to live without fear
and die without regret

We will camp here a few more days
and disappear, taking with us
every scrap of civilization we carried in,
and something more: the wild peace
of this opening in the trees,
the love song of this quiet stream,
invisible spores of a forest
that will sprout up inside us
from the dark fertile cracks
between the clicking channels of fear,
the ticking minutes of regret

We will always remember this wild
circle of faces shining in the grass,
the wild voices of these children
teaching us the secret meaning of silence,
even long after the fire-breathing machines
stop coming in to mow this meadow
and the trees close in to claim it once more...

We will never forget this wild
opening of our hearts

## Firmly Planted

Both feet firmly planted
on his skateboard,
eyes on his phone,
he rolls past my front porch
at warp speed
coasting the slight grade
of the subcontinental divide
into the cul-de-sac
with a sound like steel and asphalt
howling together
from some granite ridge
at moonrise

## To Be Human

It's wonderful to be young,
carefree, curious, footloose, flirtatious, in love—
but sooner or later you know
you'll have to grow up
and take care of your mother

*That fleeting relief, like a moment's
reprieve from gravity
whenever you drop some insignificant scrap
in the trash ...
the way a good solid tool makes you feel
less alone in the universe ...
the irresistible thrill of fresh blacktop
and a full tank of gas—
what an embarrassment to be
human
right in front of everyone!*

The housemaid,
the garbageman, the busboy—
someone has to clean up after you
every step of the way,
we're talking seven generations
of Superfund sites, and your mother
can't even change her own
diaper any more ...

Still, no matter how artificial, sterile,
stifling, wasteful, toxic
the places you live and work, you yourself
are the most undeniable
specimen of nature in the room, your will
to live as you choose
the most powerful force on Earth—

*The heart is the thing in your chest
a little left of center
that always knows what's right
and keeps on
pounding*

## The Writer on the Freeway

I too am
an internal combustion engine
panting for breath,
an oxygen-cooled, carbon-burning powerhouse
with nowhere to turn
like millions of my kind, all these
air-conditioned souls
packing the boulevards and freeways
day and night, all of us
barreling down together
on whichever doom in fact
awaits us
after centuries of prophecy and
stock-market projections,
though a few of us are
just beginning to slow down
and think about
where we're all going
so fast
and why

Against the ruin of the world, there is only one defense— the creative act.

> Kenneth Rexroth, *"Disengagement: The Art of the Beat Generation"*

# (4)
## Earth Poetry: A Manifesto

# Earth Poetry: A Manifesto
## *Reclaiming the Ecological Niche of the Poet*

### (1) The Power Song of the Shaman

Poetry in the postmodern age is a respectable branch of the entertainment industry. Among the many entertainment options in any city are anything from old-fashioned poetry readings to amateur open mikes to competitive, fast-moving poetry slams. Meanwhile, in the form of hip-hop—"spoken word" with a beat—poetry has exploded into the mainstream. And an argument can be made that the lyrics of popular music have always been a sub-genre of poetry.

But poetry has a long history, and an even longer prehistory. The roots of poetry, like those of every other modern art form, go back to the late Paleolithic, the Old Stone Age, 50,000 years ago and more. The earliest written records are barely over 5,000 years old, so for most of its long life poetry was an oral tradition, the original "spoken word," handed down through a thousand generations.

Our Paleolithic ancestors lived in nomadic tribal bands, hunting and gathering for a living, inhabiting a wild landscape shaped by glaciation and continental drift. The cave paintings, petroglyphs, stone carvings, and clay figurines they left behind on every continent are clues to a mystery. Art, these relics tell us, evolved as an essential component of human consciousness. Tools and weapons and clay vessels helped prehistoric hominids survive. But painting, sculpture, music, drama, dance, story-telling and poetry helped them to become human.

The arts were not invented for entertainment, however. Life in the Paleolithic was anything but boring. Our ancestors lived immersed in a world that was alive with danger and mystery and magic. Life was a miracle they witnessed all around them every day, and they owed their lives to the sustenance it provided. The cycles of sun, moon and stars, winter, spring, summer and fall, birth, adolescence, old age and death were interconnected parts of a larger cycle that carried them along as it turned.

We call this larger cycle *nature*, to distinguish it from what later humans have superimposed on it with our boundless, restless energy. But to prehistoric hunter-gatherers, there was no such distinction. The world was alive, it was all one, and humans were part of it— a part neither more nor less essential than the rest. They saw plants and animals, rocks and waterfalls, mountains and sky as their relatives, as indigenous people still do today, an "extended family" that extended to the stars. Dreams were an inner reflection of the mysteries they saw around them.

It was obvious to our earliest ancestors that nature was not only alive but conscious and intelligent, a belief known today as "animism." Just as they themselves lived simultaneously in the material world of the body and a non-material inner world, their nonhuman relatives— even the rocks and the waterfalls— also lived in both realms. The forces and elements of nature possessed both physical substance and an invisible inner dimension. Or, as modern physics would say, were both matter and energy, particle and wave.

Translated into English, the non-material dimension of a rock or an animal was a *spirit*— the same word still used by some for the non-material dimension of a human. The nature spirits communicated with our ancestors through dreams and through visionary experiences induced in many ways: by ingesting psychoactive plants, by fasting, by drumming, dancing and chanting. Humans communicated with the spirits in turn through ritual and art, completing the energy circuit between the inner world of dreams and the outer world of the senses.

Like nature itself, the nature spirits were not always benign. But that was another aspect of the mysterious unity of the cosmos. Sickness and health, death and birth, grief and joy were part of the balance of nature, the same cycle of changes that brought night and day, winter and summer, sunshine and storm. Ancient tribal religion honored both the creative and destructive faces of Mother Earth.

Were the nature spirits real, or only metaphorical, as the phrase "Mother Earth" is routinely used today? To the extent that language itself is an instrument made entirely of metaphors, they can be dismissed as mere archaic figures of speech. But as a poet, my task is to peer through that instrument, through the transparent but impermeable lens of words, names, definitions, grammar and syntax, and try to discern what is actually real out there in the world all creatures share.

"Animism" is just a word to us, but what it attempts to translate is a reality experienced by people who lived generation after generation in daily contact with that actual world— a world most of us today know only as the backdrop for a dog-walk, a picnic, at most a wilderness vacation. Belief in a non-material dimension populated by spirits was universal in ancient times, and still is wherever indigenous ways survive. Yet the spirit world and the world of matter were one, as inseparable as the mind and body of one being.

Science can neither prove nor disprove these beliefs, because by definition science limits itself to the visible, the tangible, the material. But what if the nature spirits inhabit a non-material fourth dimension of the three-dimensional world, counterpart to the consciousness that mysteriously inhabits the human body? What if "primitive" animistic religion was actually a sophisticated technology for contact between human consciousness and a conscious, intelligent universe, at a deep level where consciousness itself is one unified whole?

The Earth is still here, still inhabited by humans. If nature ever was conscious and intelligent, it still is. James Lovelock's Gaia Hypothesis proposes that the Earth's dazzling variety of life-forms collectively maintain optimal conditions for life on Earth. Carl Jung's concept of the collective unconscious might describe that deep place where human nature and wild nature converge. Quantum physicists are now beginning to think that consciousness itself might not be a local phenomenon produced by the human brain, but an energy field that enfolds the physical plane, analogous to the Earth's magnetic and gravitational fields. But this idea too remains unproven and, I suspect, unprovable.

As prehistoric human tribes migrated across the continents and took up residence in far-flung climates and terrains, each developed its own distinct language, religion, and mythology. But every human language had a word for the mysterious unity of birth and death, spirit and matter, nature and humankind, the all-inclusive web of relationship that weaves the cosmos into one: a word we English-speakers translate as *sacred*.

All of the arts originated not as modes of self-expression, as they are understood today, but as modes of communion with the sacred. The various genres of art were intertwined in a multimedia communal art form which today we call *ritual*. This was the origin of all religious practice. But other human activities had a sacred dimension as well. Hunting, killing, and eating an animal was an act with deep spiritual significance. Food-gathering, tool-making, mythology, ritual, art, and magic were seamlessly interwoven in a single living fabric now known as *culture*— though ours, by comparison, is splintered, disjointed, cacophonous.

Our prehistoric ancestors lived a communal life, sharing everything from storytelling under the stars to the daily work of survival. But as in every culture, individual members of the tribe were born with particular talents. Some were artists, gifted with special abilities to communicate with spirits through the creative imagination. And some were shamans, the tribal healers.

Like everything else in the ancient world, sickness and healing had a spiritual dimension. The skillful shaman could trace the physical symptoms of illness to a spiritual imbalance between the sick individual— sometimes the entire community— and the natural world. A crucial part of the healing process involved a journey to the spirit world in a dream or trance, from which the shaman would return with a song, or chant, the gift of a "spirit helper," a "power animal," a "plant ally." Shamans used herbs and other physical healing modalities in their work, but some believe it was the song that gave these modalities the power to heal. The power song of the shaman was the root of what came to be called *poetry*.

I have no idea whether an academic researcher in the field would agree with that conclusion. I'm not even sure what field it is. Fortunately, I have no professor or thesis committee to tell me I'm wrong. All I have to go on is my own experience, research, and intuition as a poet indigenous to Planet Earth.

## (2) The Path of a Wandering Poet

Unlike many who choose poetry as a vocation, I did not take the academic route through life. Foolishly, perhaps, I skipped grad school and never applied for a single writing workshop, fellowship, or literary grant. Instead, after graduating from college I hit the road to travel the country by thumb— the only graduation present I really wanted.

I'd majored in English Composition more or less by accident. When the deadline came to declare a major, I found I had already chosen one by signing up mostly for courses that allowed me to indulge my love of reading. But in all the English classes I took over 16 years of schooling, I'd never found poetry all that exciting to read. It seemed to exist in a world of its own that never quite touched mine. As an English major I learned to scan its meter, map its rhyme scheme, analyze its symbolism, decipher its literary allusions, and write a convincing term paper relating its themes and motifs to the historical backdrop or literary pedigree of the poet. I wrote the poems assigned to me in creative writing class, though not exactly on deadline, and even took a semester-length course in poetry-writing.

But I never took an interest in actually reading all those poets I had studied until I unexpectedly wrote a poem no one had assigned me to write, and discovered it was possible to write lines and stanzas about something I really cared about: poetry that actually *meant something*, at least to me. The poem that took me by surprise was about hitchhiking— my spiritual path, my graduate school, my chosen career.

From that point on, I was a poet. The poems I wrote were lousy, of course. But if one persists in writing poems, one is indisputably a poet. And the more I wrote, the more curious I grew about what other poets might be doing with the skills and tools I was gradually developing. I still have the battered copies of Whitman, Pound, Yeats, Gary Snyder and Galway Kinnell that rode around the country with me in my backpack.

The only poem I wrote during those years that still speaks to me is one I wrote on a canoe trip after an up-close encounter with a loon. In the summer after ninth grade I had signed up for a church-sponsored summer camp program and discovered the Boundary Waters— an unspoiled wilderness of glacier-carved lakes on the Minnesota-Ontario border. I eagerly signed up again every summer all the way through high school as a camper, again through my college years as a camp counselor, and even as co-director of a couple of trips after that, responsible for bringing a dozen teenagers back from the wilderness alive.

That annual trip to the North Woods awoke something in me which slowly, summer by summer, became my spiritual core. Which was ironic, because during those same years I was drifting away from the liberal Protestant Christianity I had grown up with. Looking back now, I recognize that what I experienced out in the wilderness, under the auspices of the United Methodist church, was not a religious conversion but a spiritual awakening.

"Creation," I saw with growing clarity, was not something given to humans for human purposes, but a living miracle with its own purpose and meaning, suffused with a divine intelligence that could not be described in scriptures or doctrines or creeds. In Sunday School I had learned about a God who kicked people out of a Garden to wander in the wilderness— then later led their descendants out of the wilderness into a Promised Land. But my own Promised Land was incorruptibly wild; my Garden was preserved in its original condition, innocent of Original Sin.

My post-college hitchhiking trip stretched into a twelve-year odyssey around the country, Eventually I married and settled in Atlanta, found a job, volunteered in various activist causes, joined the boards of two nonprofits. Though I never stopped writing poems, sharing them, and periodically submitting them to magazines and journals, recognition as a poet never ranked among my highest goals in life.

During my travels I wrote more poems about hitchhiking, and years later published a book of them. I discovered the Rainbow Gathering, an annual encampment in the National Forests dedicated to world peace and neo-tribal community. When I moved to Georgia, far from the Boundary Waters, this became my annual pilgrimage to the woods. I wrote poems about the Gatherings, and when the Gathering finally came to Georgia I published a book of those, too, as a crowdfunded giveaway. I wrote love poems, poems about family, protest poems about poverty and racism and war. But as I matured, my relationship to nature deepened. The time I spent in the woods became increasingly precious, and nature became a consistent theme in the poetry I was writing.

Eventually I noticed that the same theme cropped up repeatedly in the poetry I was reading as well. The literary traditions of every culture and period, I realized, had produced poets who wrote about nature. Nature appeared as image, as metaphor, as myth, as a source of wisdom and inspiration, as direct experience or vivid dream. Poets regarded the natural world with awe and gratitude, mourned and raged against its desecration at human hands, used it as a springboard for metaphysical speculation or surrealistic free association.

Had this phenomenon ever been studied by graduate students in English literature? I didn't know, and in that backward age before the internet, I didn't know how to find out. But it seemed to me a significant discovery. I decided to call it "Earth poetry."

## (3) The Whispers of Nature Spirits

Although poetry from its very beginnings played a vital role in the communal life of the tribe, the power song originated as a communication from the nature spirits to an individual person, the shaman. The poem therefore represented a message to the human community from the natural world, channeled through a particular chosen individual, and was respected and valued as such by the tribe.

The poet and Zen practitioner Gary Snyder, whose undergraduate degree was in anthropology, sums up the shamanic legacy of poetry this way: "The philosopher, poet, and yogin all three have standing not too far behind them the shaman; with his or her pelt and antlers, or various other guises; songs going back to the Pleistocene and before. The shaman speaks for wild animals, the spirits of plants, the spirits of mountains, of watersheds. He or she sings for them. They sing through him. This capacity has often been achieved via special disciplines." (*The Old Ways*, "The Yogin & the Philosopher," p.12)

I get a taste of how this feels at the Rainbow Gathering. The poems about past Gatherings I share around the campfire, though otherwise only pale ghosts of a traditional power song, echo the tribal function of the shaman in one key respect. They celebrate the communal bonding that makes the Gathering work on a human level, but they also honor the natural setting that silently encourages that deeply buried tribal consciousness to emerge. For this I feel respected and valued, like others who serve the more pragmatic needs of the Gathering— though I also try to do my share of the work. Performing my poetry in any room where people have gathered specifically to listen, I feel a certain ego-gratification. But in the forest, in the flicker of firelight, it's not only the human listeners who give me that special tingle, but the breeze, the starlight, the surrounding trees, the fire itself.

Over the millennia, as humankind spread and proliferated and diversified, poets and bards and griots inherited the sacred function of the shaman in human society. But human society was changing, developing in drastically different ways in different regions of the globe. Some cultures retained their indigenous beliefs and rely on shamans for healing to this day. In others, little by little an attitude of dominance and exploitation gradually replaced the ancient sense of nature as one extended family.

Some 12,000 years ago, the Paleolithic began to give way to the agricultural Neolithic: the New Stone Age. As herding and farming peoples domesticated the animals and plants their ancestors had hunted and gathered, religious practice gradually shifted to the worship of supernatural entities, and hierarchical orders of priests took over the shaman's task of contact with the sacred. Each culture had its gods and goddesses, but the divinity of the Earth itself was not forgotten. Throughout the ancient world, under many names, a great Mother Goddess personified the mysterious oneness of seedtime and harvest, of giving birth and dying, of the maiden, mother, and wise old crone phases of life. Poets sang her praises in cycles of ritual through the moons and seasons.

The domesticated villagers of agrarian society slowly began to see themselves as separate from and superior to the natural world. But at the deep level of dreams and visions, the human psyche's relationship with nature remained intact. As human concepts of the sacred changed, the nature spirits adopted new disguises and continued to whisper in the ears of poets. The magical spell, the meditation mantra, the *Tao Te Ching*, *The Iliad* and *The Odyssey*, the Hebrew Psalms, the *bhakti* chants of India, the Arabic *ghazal*, the Zen *koan*, the Methodist hymnal, and all the schools and movements of poetry through the ages are descendants of the power songs brought back from the spirit world by ancient tribal shamans.

As the early civilizations of Mesopotamia, Egypt, China, India, and Mesoamerica further consolidated human control over nature, beginning around 6,000 years ago, the shape of the sacred in human culture followed suit. The gods and goddesses of the various pagan pantheons still embodied the forces and elements of nature, but in a more anthropocentric form. The human heroes of past ages were deified; the rulers of empires proactively declared themselves divine as well. Meanwhile, the revolutionary new technology of the written word was expanding beyond its original function of keeping track of accounts. Myths and epics that had been told and retold around countless campfires were finally written down by poets like Homer and Hesiod in Greece and the Hebrew scribes of Israel, who were semi-mythical figures themselves.

Still later, as more and more of the world's peoples were overpowered and absorbed into warlike empires, including the monotheistic theocracies of Europe and the Middle East— a process historians call "civilization"— the manyfold whispers of nature merged into one unified voice. Whether people called it Yahweh, Buddha, Allah, the Tao, the Beloved, the Christ, the message was oneness, the eternal essence of the sacred. Sometimes a whisper was not enough: the message came in a clap of thunder, a blinding light, a burning bush, a visionary experience that human prophets and mystics could not ignore.

Unfortunately, transcribing and interpreting the message was left to the priests, scribes, and temple bureaucrats— the literate class— who served the rulers. The "oneness" these officials exalted as supreme began to exclude nature and its "heathen" deities, along with animals and plants, women, sexuality, the physical body itself, certain skin tones deemed less than human. The illiterate faithful who had once revered the sacredness of nature now transferred their veneration to the official "sacred texts."

In his "Proverbs of Hell," William Blake described how the wild imagination had been domesticated, step by step: "The ancient Poets animated all sensible objects with Gods or Geniuses, calling them by the names and adorning them with the properties of woods, rivers, mountains, lakes, cities, nations, and whatever their enlarged & numerous senses could perceive ... Till a system was formed, which some took advantage of & enslav'd the vulgar by attempting to realize or abstract the mental deities from their objects: thus began Priesthood. Choosing forms of worship from poetic tales. And at length they pronounced that the Gods had orderd such things. Thus men forgot that All deities reside in the human breast." (*The Marriage of Heaven & Hell*, Plate 11).

Still, in every age and language, the nature spirits went on whispering in the ears of poets. In imperial China, where indigenous spirituality was embedded in Taoist philosophy, poetry was the most popular literary genre by far. Poets like Li Po, Tu Fu, Wang Wei, and Han Shan were quoted and honored. Most held positions in the vast bureaucracy of the Emperors, and wrote their poetry during getaways to mountain retreats. Nature was a constant theme, both as a consolation for the sorrows of life and as a reminder of the transience of joy.

In Japan, influenced by the indigenous Shinto religion, the Zen Buddhists found in poetry an apt way to express the insights of interpenetration— the oneness of all things— and impermanence, the endless cycles of change. Poets like Basho, Issa, and Buson were renowned for their *haiku*, capturing in 17 evocative syllables the age-old resonance between human lives and the changing seasons. In the 16th century, writing *haiku* became a national obsession among the common people of Japan, and it remains popular today.

In medieval Europe, under the Christian doctrine of "dominion" over nature, the worship of the Great Goddess was forced underground— only to surface in a new disguise, the mythology of the poet's Muse. She was the goddess of the romantic ideal, of archetypal Woman. But she was also Mother Earth, ancient and eternal, and she spoke through the troubadours of French Provence, among others. Mystics like Hildegard of Bingen in Germany and Jalal al-Din Rumi in Turkey expressed their visions of oneness in poetic metaphor to avoid being branded as heretics by their respective religious authorities.

With the rise of the Industrial Revolution in Europe, religion began to lose its pre-eminence as wealthy capitalists developed ever more efficient methods of exploiting nature. Under the philosophical influence of the Enlightenment, poetry became an intellectual exercise with little connection to nature. Beginning with Blake in the late 1700s, a younger generation of poets known today as the Romantics rebelled against the view of nature as nothing more than raw material for civilization's ideal of "progress." In England the Romantics included John Keats, William Wordsworth, and Lord Byron; in Europe, Gerard de Nerval, Friedrich Holderlin, and Johann Wilhelm von Goethe. In the United States, Emily Dickinson and Walt Whitman joined the rebellion in a uniquely American vernacular.

In the 20th century, when mainstream poetry left tradition behind and launched an era of "modernist" exploration, once again a rebellious few carried on the sacred task of representing wild nature in the human world. In the U.S. they included Robinson Jeffers, Theodore Roethke, Kenneth Rexroth, Denise Levertov, James Wright, Galway Kinnell, W.S. Merwin, Gary Snyder, Wendell Berry, and Mary Oliver, to name only a few. It was from that generation of poets— my tribal elders— that I learned my craft.

What I call "Earth poetry" is only one strand in the rich weave of poetic traditions and innovations around the world. But virtually every book of poetry I have ever dipped into or devoured is infused with nature imagery and metaphor to some extent, from the ancient Greeks to the postmodern avant-garde. This is no surprise. Our indigenous past lives on in our DNA; it's only natural that people who are in touch with their inner selves at the deepest level will receive occasional communications from the nature spirits, whether they consciously experience it that way or not.

Unfortunately, humankind has ignored the message, misinterpreted the prophets, deified the soulless dollar, and relegated poetry to the realm of entertainment. The nature spirits have given up whispering; they are roaring now, keening, moaning, raging, clamoring for our attention. Plastic-choked oceans, clearcut forests, depleted topsoil and aquifers, mass extinction and climate chaos cry out to be heard. But those in power seem to hear nothing but the cash registers ringing in their ears. Nature herself will survive, naturally. But suddenly the destiny of humankind is up for grabs.

## (4) The Revival of the Sacred

The mathematical odds of a world like ours coming to be through sheer chance are so astronomical that even an astronomer might use the word "miraculous"— metaphorically, of course. But whether you believe the Earth and all its myriad life-forms evolved over five billion years by a process of mutation and adaptation, or were created in six days by a benevolent deity, you will probably agree that a liveable planet is rare enough that it should be kept liveable at all costs. Especially if it happens to be the planet that makes our own lives liveable.

The word *sacred* is normally used in a religious context. But I propose a broader meaning. Anything we utterly depend on to continue living and breathing— not to mention the potentially endless generations to come— can and should be regarded as sacred, regardless of world-view and belief-system. Tampering with the life support systems of Planet Earth ought to be taboo, and in many religious traditions it is.

More and more people are coming to the same conclusion, among them the Dalai Lama, Pope Francis I, and a wave of evangelical Christians who consider themselves stewards of God's Creation. Indigenous people, schoolchildren, activists of every description are sounding the alarm. Even scientists are beginning to peel off the spotless white coat of neutral objectivity to advocate for wilderness conservation, ecosystem restoration, renewable energy, nuclear disarmament, a proactive stance toward climate change.

The evolutionary future of our species, like any other, requires that we place the highest value on maximizing the next generation's chances of survival. Regarding our own comfort and convenience as more precious than the future of our children is pure insanity. In biological terms, it is evolutionary suicide. Awakening the human community to this obvious truth is the key to surviving the multiple interlocking environmental emergencies we face today.

Unfortunately, poets cannot rescue humankind from organized, efficient, well-funded human folly all by ourselves. But we do have a role to play. Like the shaman's, it is a role of healing, of connection, of bringing the voice of nature into the cultural conversation. By reviving the original function of poetry in human society, we can help to catalyze the mass awakening that is so sorely needed. Poets are uniquely equipped to supply the missing link between humans and the biosphere that feeds us: the perspective of the sacred.

But to speak of the sacred in today's polarized society is likely to offend the religious and alienate the secular, further dividing us instead of bringing the human tribe together in defense of its own future. Luckily, the word itself is merely shorthand for a miraculous oneness which is still visible wherever we turn. Whether the scenery is wild or pastoral, suburban or urban, nature is omnipresent and alive as ever.

As alternatives to statistics and data, the Earth poet offers imagery and inspiration. Imagery of nature's beauty, from the geometry of a seashell to the grandeur of a canyon; inspiration arising in response from that deep level where human nature is still wild, still capable of perceiving what is sacred. Earth poetry sees the miracle of Creation not as mere metaphor, nor as a literal act of God, but as a third kind of miracle: a world where spirit and matter mingle and interplay, reveal themselves in the light of one another— and occasionally fuse together in a sudden vision of oneness.

But here in the 21st century, can a miracle as vast as the starry universe be seen with the naked eye? An eye hooked on the split-second editing and special effects of a digital screen? An eye trained to see the world through an electron microscope, a spectrometer, a radiotelescope? A poem can offer a poet's perspective, but can it persuade people to *see*? Can it convey to modern humans a sense of the sacred, not in the traditional religious sense, but in the sense of awe and wonder that was the original seed of religion itself?

This, ladies and gentlemen, is where the poet as entertainer takes the stage. Our shamanic heritage has not only a religious function but a magical one. Through the link to the nonhuman realm that all humans share— the wild imagination— Earth poets can cast a potent spell in luminous, musical language, countering the spell cast by a thousand channels of distraction, the seductive enchantment of irrelevance. We can invite all who read or listen into the sacred dimension of life on Earth without so much as whispering the word.

Standing just outside the human realm and looking in, singing our power songs, we can entice our readers or listeners to step out of the human melodrama and re-connect with the larger drama that goes on around us, regardless of human plans and priorities. Migrating geese and salmon and Monarch butterflies. The slow journey of forest succession toward climax. The stubborn survival of keystone species like wolves and grizzlies. Sightings of deer and coyotes in urban neighborhoods. The unstoppable trickles and torrents of water, erosion and deposition, evaporation and rainfall. And the heroism of humans restoring waterways and re-planting forests— this is a form of natural beauty, too.

Earth poetry is not "nature poetry," poetry about nature, but poetry about *our relationship* with nature— not as tourists or spectators or scientists, but as conscious participants in a living world. Venturing beyond the fortified borders of the human ego, Earth poets are moved not only to wonder and gratitude for nature's gifts, but to grief and rage for every lost species, coral reef, old-growth forest. My feelings do not speak for others, but might remind them of long-buried and forgotten feelings of their own.

Practitioners of a branch of psychotherapy called "ecopsychology" trace today's pandemic of ailments like depression, anxiety, addiction, and random violence to a society-wide suppression of feelings of love and loss for the world we are collectively ravaging in the name of progress. Like the shamans, these therapists have taken on the task of healing a spiritual imbalance between the human and natural worlds, restoring a lost connection that has left humans themselves feeling lost. Some eco-psychologists have even brought shamanic techniques into their practices.

Poets too have inherited the shamanic legacy of healing the rift between the worlds. But where therapy focuses primarily on the individual, poetry speaks to society as a whole. The ancient shamans communicated with spirits not just to heal a sick individual, but on behalf of the entire tribe. Earth poets, too, bring back from the spirit world— from our own deeply personal relationships with nature— a gift for the human tribe. Our gift, too, takes the form of song: the rhythm of breath and heartbeat, the truth of heartfelt emotion, the vision of re-connection with our extended family of nonhuman relatives and our deepest selves.

Society is made up of individuals, of course, and the fundamental connection of any art form is person to person, heart to heart. In the right time and place, the right poem can awaken in a listening heart the possibility, the seed— no matter how small— of a personal relationship with nature. But that seed can only thrive in the context of community, our modern-day approximation of the tribal society in which humankind originally sprouted and grew.

The isolation of the individual is a modern phenomenon, the inevitable outcome of our long exile from nature. Therapy can't heal people trapped in a sick society; that requires the medicine of community. Just as Paleolithic art did in the context of ritual, Earth poetry can bring people together to experience the sacred— the oneness of body, mind, heart, spirit, community, cosmos. It's this experience of oneness at every level that heals.

## (5) The Voice of What Truly Matters

To take this sacred charge seriously, Earth poets need to ask ourselves why poetry's market-share in the entertainment industry is so small. What is it that restricts the appeal of mainstream poetry to an elite, educated audience? Why is the poetry published in *The New Yorker* and so many literary journals intentionally cryptic, frivolous, obscure, disengaged with real issues and devoid of real emotion? I wonder if it's because poetry has lost its "voice"— not literally, but in the literary sense of the term; not the personal voice of the poet, but the poetic persona that speaks through the poem.

Until about a century ago, reading and reciting poetry was a popular pastime among ordinary folks. With a few exceptions, such as Wordsworth and Whitman, most poetry of that era used rocking-horse rhythms and merry-go-round rhymes that made it easy to memorize, and spoke in its own specialized language: the poetic "voice." What people expected from a good poem was formal diction, stilted syntax, flowery phrases, alliteration and assonance, melodramatic themes, ostentatious symbolism, allusions to classical literature and mythology. These flourishes served to set the poet's voice apart from the prosaic day-to-day, giving it a loftier, more authoritative seat from which to observe and expound. But to the modern ear, this antiquated style sounds pompous and artificial.

After World War I, a new epoch abruptly arrived. Tradition everywhere came crashing down, blown asunder by the horrors of technological advances in the conduct of war. Under the influence of modernists like T.S. Eliot, Ezra Pound, and Wallace Stevens, poets began to experiment. Rhyme and meter went out of fashion— along with the custom of saying something coherent in a poem. Painting and sculpture, music, drama and dance underwent a similar mutation, reflecting the shattered conventions of meaning. Literature increasingly became an academic specialty. Literary criticism elevated poetry above the pastime for common folk it had always been. Poets responded with poems that were more and more intellectual, abstract, and surreal. Poetry was growing up, and like a hormone-flooded adolescent, its "voice" was changing.

The new voice spoke with the authority of an exhilarating new age of individual freedom. It was the voice of dazzling originality, unleashed imagination, sheer reckless possibility. In the place of poetic convention, the modernist poets celebrated invention. What set the new poetic voice apart from the prosaic day-to-day of the new century was its daring, its edge: language and imagery and a shape on the page that defied rational sense, painting in abstract colors a realistic portrait of an irrational world. Readers found no trace of old-fashioned message or meaning in poems that cynically depicted— while helping to create— a newly meaningless universe. T.S. Eliot's hugely influential "The Waste Land" bravely mapped a new frontier of alienation and despair. But people adrift in a meaningless world *yearn* for meaning . . . and poetry began to lose the mass audience it had long enjoyed.

Like many of my peers, I went through various phases of imitation as I discovered one by one the poets who pioneered the schools, styles, and movements of the 20th century. I too wrote poems in secret code— poetry that cloaked its meaning, if it meant anything, in whimsical wordplay, elaborate metaphor, hallucinogenic imagery, random leaps between disconnected thoughts. These experiments in poetic possibility were gloriously legitimate in their day, when the human imagination was expanding, exploring, bursting out of the husk of tradition in order to fly free.

But now we have reached a plateau where we can look back over the centuries, over the clutter of obsolete technologies and crumbling monuments, and assess what civilization has given us— including this joyous freedom to experiment— and what it has cost. What civilization has given us, we are beginning to see, has very nearly cost us our children's future. It is time now to speak plainly of what is real and what is not. It is time to write about what we truly care about, in language that conveys clear meaning. The days of veiled abstraction and surreal fancy are over, like the days of meter and rhyme before them. Poetic conceits and arbitrary technique will now only get in the way.

In the the 21st-century literary world, declaring that poetry must *mean something* is tantamount to heresy. The critics and professors will have nothing to decipher! But maybe the hip-hop artists and the singer-songwriters know something poets have forgotten. Maybe the size of their market-share has to do not just with synthesized beats and guitar solos, but with an unabashed willingness to *say something*, and to say it in plain language, no matter how trivial or trite. Maybe poetry needs a new voice— something to set it apart from the prosaic day-to-day of a technologically-driven dystopia which is rapidly laying waste to its resource base, contaminating its water supply, and sending a once-stable climate spinning out of control.

Between the extremes of classical formalism and a formless freedom de-coupled from meaning lies the path of plain language: a voice that is truthful, imaginative, original, grounded in honest emotion and a deep connection to the living world. Like the voice of a preacher, it draws from a well of moral authority. But rather than the chapter and verse of scripture, Earth poetry's authority springs from the childish innocence of our love for the land and its creatures.

Of course, if the poet tries to preach, if the poetic voice is too earnest and humorless, its readers and listeners will turn back to the voices of diversion, distraction and denial. The power song of the shaman sings not of morality, of good and evil, but of balance, of the oneness underlying all opposition and conflict. Poetry must entertain, but it can no longer afford to distract. It must bring to our attention, in sharp focus, our responsibility as adults to the innocent young of every species.

## (6) The Rise of the Ecopoets

When the Digital Age arrived, I eventually got around to searching the internet for "Earth poetry." I found lists of inspirational poems for Earth Day; places to post a favorite poem; a do-it-yourself site where visitors can contribute to a "community poem"; illustrated posters that read like oversized greeting cards; a host of flowery love-letters to Mother Earth that reminded me of my own awkward beginnings as a poet. I even found an old brochure I had once designed to publicize my workshops. Earth poetry is clearly alive and thriving among the population at large, plain-spoken enough, but mostly lacking the depth and energy of a shamanic power song.

A search for "eco-poetry," on the other hand, took me to the other end of the spectrum— an erudite 2016 essay by John Shoptaw, a poet and professor at the University of California, published on the Poetry Foundation website. His definition is simple enough: to qualify, an "ecopoem" must be both *environmental* and *environmentalist*.

"By environmental," he writes, "I mean first that an ecopoem needs to be about the nonhuman natural world— wholly or partly, in some way or other, but really and not just figuratively." To me, in contrast, the figurative references to nature that appear so often in poetry are natural outcroppings of *human* nature, the vestige of wild ancestry that lurks in our DNA and provides an unconscious landscape for the wanderings of the creative imagination. Metaphors drawn from nature demonstrate that human nature is deeply rooted in its original habitat, and the subterranean channel that connects them is open both ways. Rather than drawing a boundary between the human and nonhuman worlds, Earth poetry is about drawing them together again.

But like me, Shoptaw makes a separate category of "nature poetry." Quoting the "ecological poetics" of poet and essayist Forrest Gander, he distinguishes nature poetry from "poetry that investigates— both thematically and formally— the relationship between nature and culture, language and perception." I applaud the emphasis on "relationship," but the relationship I reach for in my poems is not so much thematic and formal as personal and emotional, heartfelt, sensual, visceral.

Shoptaw himself sees the difference in terms of the poem's relationship to the reader, rather than to nature: "Ecopoetry is nature poetry that has designs on us, that imagines changing the ways we think, feel about, and live and act in the world." This is the *environmentalist* aspect of eco-poetry; it portrays an environment that is, "implicitly or explicitly, impacted by humans," but goes beyond an aesthetic portrayal to spur readers and listeners to concern, even to action. By contrast, a poem purely about nature's impact on humans, whether aesthetic, psychological, or spiritual, is just a nature poem. In fact, writing about nature without mentioning the hovering threat of ecological ruin verges on complacency, even "immorality."

Dwelling too heavily on the human menace, however, runs the opposite risk of "moralizing." Ecopoetry cannot become didactic, Shoptaw says, reduced to a blunt object for teaching one more "tiresome lesson" about guilt and duty. This is a delicate line to draw, since the effect of any given poem is as varied as its readers. I too welcome an activist stance in an Earth poem, but that is only one of the myriad ways nature speaks through poetry. Each poem will naturally take a different form, shaped by the poet's perspective and experience of a particular place and time. Defining an ecopoem as not only *environmental* but *environmentalist* further narrows its scope.

For me, the heart of Shoptaw's piece is his summary of ecopoet Jorie Graham's thoughts on didacticism in an interview with *Earthlines* magazine. From the range of potential readers Graham singles out the ones who "feel anything remotely 'political' to be polemical and thus didactic. They feel they 'know this information already, so why do they need it in a poem.' That," Graham emphasizes, "is precisely the point. They 'know' it. They are not 'feeling it.' That is what activists in the environmental movement are asking of us: help it be felt, help it be imagined." Bravo! Feeling and imagining are precisely what we need to break through the paralysis of so much demoralizing information.

I also admired Shoptaw's defense of the poetic device of "anthropomorphization"– depicting an animal, for instance, as a character with human-like motives who thinks and acts like us. This imaginative communion between species is a revival of an ancient magical practice, routine for any Paleolithic shaman dancing in a wolf skin or elk antlers, and a staple of folk tales and mythology from traditional cultures the world over. The shamans and storytellers, of course, would be intimately familiar with the species they portrayed. But imagination has its roots in magic, and no one can say for sure that a poet's animal allies are not whispering through the poem. Again, the goal is not literary correctness, but to reach the reader somewhere deep enough to open a channel of communion with the wild.

Though I enjoyed soaking up Shoptaw's professional expertise, I'm very much an outsider in his world. If I were to keep on sniffing my way through the digital universe, as I obviously should, I'm sure I would unearth many more choice encounters like this, explore many unsuspected avenues, meet many kindred spirits, deepen my own knowledge, and perhaps end up feeling my notion of "Earth poetry" is altogether redundant.

But what troubled me as I read, with one exception, were the examples Shoptaw chose to illustrate his insightful and thought-provoking points— the snippets of contemporary poetry he held up as exemplary ecopoems. I had to scratch my head, wondering: *Who are these poets talking to? Who are they writing for?* My best guess is: *Each other.* They all come out of the closed-door culture of the writing workshop, I suspect, where budding writers critique each other, strive to impress each other, spur each other on to new feats of derring-do, but never ask for feedback from the janitor pushing a broom out in the hall.

The mission of ecopoetry as a subgenre seems to mirror the apparent aspiration of contemporary poetry as a whole: writing not to communicate, to be read, heard, and understood—in any sense of that word—but to construct arcane puzzles of words, playing hide and seek with images and metaphors. It's the toothless and tottering century-old culture of innovation, desperate not to repeat itself, disdainful of the simple reality of feelings that all humans share, afraid to trust in the inherent originality of the unique individual with something to say.

The one exception I mentioned is Robert Hass's poem "Ezra Pound's Proposition," a powerful but flawed depiction of the causes and effects of a dam-building project in Thailand. It literally sent electric shivers up my spine— once I made it past the opening lines, which are apparently an actual account of the genesis of the poem in Hass's mind. When propositioned by a teenaged prostitute in Bangkok, evidently his *very first thought* was of a line from Pound's *Cantos* about economics and fertility. Yes, I did get the pun, though without a graduate degree in English literature it took me a minute. But what is the point of taking me there before commencing the actual business of the poem? To drive away readers unqualified to read further? Or just to demonstrate the poet's intellectual prowess? It's a perfect example of the poet getting in the way of the poem.

After all of Shoptaw's exclusionary clauses, however, his bottom line is not about defending academic turf but about defending the Earth. "An ecopoem may be innovative or it may be what I call 'renovative' (where any poetic feature, past or present, is available for renewal), or it may even be resolutely traditionalist— and it may appear anywhere. We need all kinds of poems to find and stir up all sorts of poetry readers." This certainly includes

Hass's many admirers, whose taste is obviously more sophisticated than mine. I can only be grateful that the ecopoets are out there working the field next to mine, and be thankful for occasional gaps in the fence.

In the bars and coffeehouses, meanwhile, the slam poets and the amateur rappers and the retro-beatniks are lining up for their chance at the microphone. The many open mikes I have attended over the years have unfailingly showcased the depth and range of poetry that wells up continuously and unstoppably from the aquifers of the wild imagination, with or without the benefit of professors and workshops. Because most of us nowadays are city folks, these otherwise diverse poets are almost exclusively concerned with the dramas and traumas of the human world. But their overriding emphasis is to communicate, bravely sharing their private worlds in the public domain, going deep within to bring back a gift from the unconscious for the human tribe. This is the real cutting edge of the ancient legacy of the shamans.

## (7) The Gifts of the Wild Imagination

Personally, I have never had a visionary experience, even during the acid trips of yore. I rarely even remember my dreams. I don't practice meditation or go mountaineering. I never learned to identify more than a few birds, trees, stars or constellations. I live in an urban neighborhood, not off-grid in the deep woods. At best, I escape the city to pitch my tent in the forest three or four times a year. I have never attempted a "vision quest." I can claim no shamanic training or initiation, and I can't *swear* that a nature spirit ever actually whispered in my ear.

What I do know is that suspiciously often, while I'm camping out in the woods or sitting in my back yard, a phrase will pop into my head and I will faithfully jot it down. It can happen on a city sidewalk too, just as it used to on the highway shoulder. These are the seeds of poems. They are my spontaneous response to whatever I imagine I hear nature whispering, mysteriously surfacing from my spiritual core, my sense of belonging here on Earth, nurtured by nature's abundance.

Some of these spontaneous seeds will sprout and grow until they fill a page or more. Others turn out to be random pieces of a poem slowly taking shape in my subconscious. Still others are complete exactly as I jotted them down. This book is the harvest of four decades of such moments, a transcript of my ongoing conversation with the wild. If nothing else, they demonstrate the surprising range of responses our multifaceted planet is capable of inspiring. Whether or not they live up to the aspirations expressed in this essay is for you to decide.

Like many a poet and artist before me, I am reluctant to take credit for these gifts from the wild imagination. On the other hand, I have to be grateful. Even after thirty years of domesticated life, of marriage and work and paying off a mortgage, I still feel a tiny bit wild myself: the youthful hitchhiker somehow captured and caged, dazed and bewildered, wondering how it happened and where the decades have gone. Earth poetry frees that wild part of me to prowl the night and sing to the moon.

My style and subject matter do not seem to suit the literary journals. More often my work has appeared in niche magazines like *Communities*, *Sojourners*, *Creation Spirituality*, and *Mothering*. I have published or self-published four books of poetry and numerous chapbooks, and performed for a variety of audiences in my decidedly non-theatrical style. And for over a decade I have hosted a quarterly "Earth Poetry" workshop, inviting other poets to join me in exploring the many nature preserves of metropolitan Atlanta. My coffee-table book *Wild Atlanta* collects the poems I have brought home from these expeditions, illuminated by Luz Wright's exquisite photos of each place.

Labeling myself an "Earth poet" is a tad pretentious, I realize. Sometimes to my own ear my work sounds too polished, too pointed, too obvious. I know I should be sly and indirect, allude rather than allege, let my readers make the leap instead of leading them there. But the time to raise awareness and inspire action is short, and the stakes are high. I have given up trying to domesticate my own nature; I accept myself as I am, as I naturally think and feel and write, and I write down whatever comes out. I am nature, like you, and nature knows what it's doing.

Robert Graves, a poet of the old school, survived combat in World War I but stubbornly carried on the traditions of meter and rhyme. His poetic vision was even more old-school: "The function of poetry is religious invocation of the Muse; its use is the experience of mixed exaltation and horror that her presence excites. But 'nowadays'? Function and use remain the same; only the application has changed. This was once a warning to man that he must keep in harmony with the family of living creatures among which he was born, by obedience to the wishes of the lady of the house; it is now a reminder that he has disregarded the warning, turned the house upside down by capricious experiments in philosophy, science and industry, and brought ruin on himself and his family." (*The White Goddess*, p.14)

Ruin might indeed turn out to be the end of the story ... but the ending has yet to be written. Every one of us has something to say about that, a vital contribution no one else can offer. Too many are numbed by denial, cauterized by grief, paved over by despair, desperately filling with consumption and addiction the bottomless hole where a close, reciprocal feeling of connection to land and sea and sky belongs. But if enough of us wake up in time to nature's warning, together we just might achieve the critical mass that is needed for large-scale transformation.

At this point, that looks unlikely; statistical probability is not on our side. Earth poetry is not going to miraculously go viral and enlighten the masses. But political activism alone will not turn the tide, either. What gives me hope is the multitude of activists who are committed enough to keep going in the face of statistical probabilities. Activists like these are motivated deeply from within; the nature spirits are whispering to them, too. If anything can save us, it will be a commitment that springs from that deep place. A rising awareness of what is real and what is not: a contagious solidarity with life in all its myriad forms: a dawning vision of the sacred. "Water is Life," after all, was not just a slogan of the heroic Water Protectors at Standing Rock, but a seed-kernel of sacred poetry.

Earth poetry is one of many paths that humans have explored in the age-long search for our original state of oneness with nature, the deep human longing for reunion with the cosmos. In our time, this is not just a spiritual quest. It is an urgent practical necessity. Down in the wild depths of the psyche, where dreams and imagination and long-suppressed feelings ache to be released, the living planet that birthed us waits to welcome us home— this sunlit, spinning miracle that gives us life and breath and sustenance, whether we look down and notice it or not.

*Stephen Wing*

## About the Author

Stephen Wing discovered the wilderness in the summer after ninth grade, traveling by canoe through the Boundary Waters of Minnesota, and suddenly the world made sense. A deep connection to wild nature has been his spiritual center ever since. The son of Methodist missionaries, he grew up in Southeast Asia and returned to the States in 1970 to attend high school in the Chicago suburbs and earn a writing degree at Beloit College. He spent his twenties traveling the country by thumb. In 1990 he met his wife, Dawn Aura, and gave up a dream of living in the woods to settle in Atlanta.

Yet even there, he found, nature is everywhere, and always wild. For over a decade he has hosted his "Earth Poetry" workshop once each season, exploring Atlanta's many protected urban wildspaces. In 2023 he was awarded a grant from the city's Office of Cultural Affairs to publish WILD ATLANTA: GREENSPACES & NATURE PRESERVES OF 'THE CITY IN THE FOREST,' a coffee-table book celebrating 23 parks and nature preserves, with color photographs by Luz Wright.

Wing is has also published three other books of poems, the Earth Poetry chapbook series, and an e-book about recycling, BETWEEN CLEANLINESS & GODLINESS, as well as a line of bumper stickers, "Gaia-Love Graffiti." He has completed two novels of his projected trilogy KUMBU'S GIFT, a comedy with an environmental theme (publisher queries welcome!) and writes a monthly blog called "Wingtips."

During his years in Atlanta Wing worked first at a wholesale book distributor, then at his neighborhood food co-op, coordinating the recycling at both companies. In 2006 he became a grateful cancer survivor. Now retired, he serves on the boards of the Lake Claire Community Land Trust and Nuclear Watch South. To read more of Wing's writings, download his e-book, watch a video rendition of this book's title poem, subscribe to his blog, or contact him about his workshops, talks, and readings, please visit his website:

### www.StephenWing.com

## COLOPHON

Prospera, the primary font used throughout this book, was the first typeface to be designed entirely on a personal computer. It was created by my good friend Peter Fraterdeus in the late 1980s with the assistance of a grant from the National Endowment for the Arts. Its debut appearance in a printed book was my first poetry collection in 1992, and I have used it in all my publications since. Sadly, we lost Peter at age 66 to an inoperable brain tumor in the fall of 2019. His inspired calligraphy and other artwork live on at www.fraterdeus.com.

www.ingramcontent.com/pod-product-compliance
Lightning Source LLC
Chambersburg PA
CBHW070527010526
44110CB00050B/2182